WRITING WITH A

EXPOSITORY WRITING

—Writing to Explain—

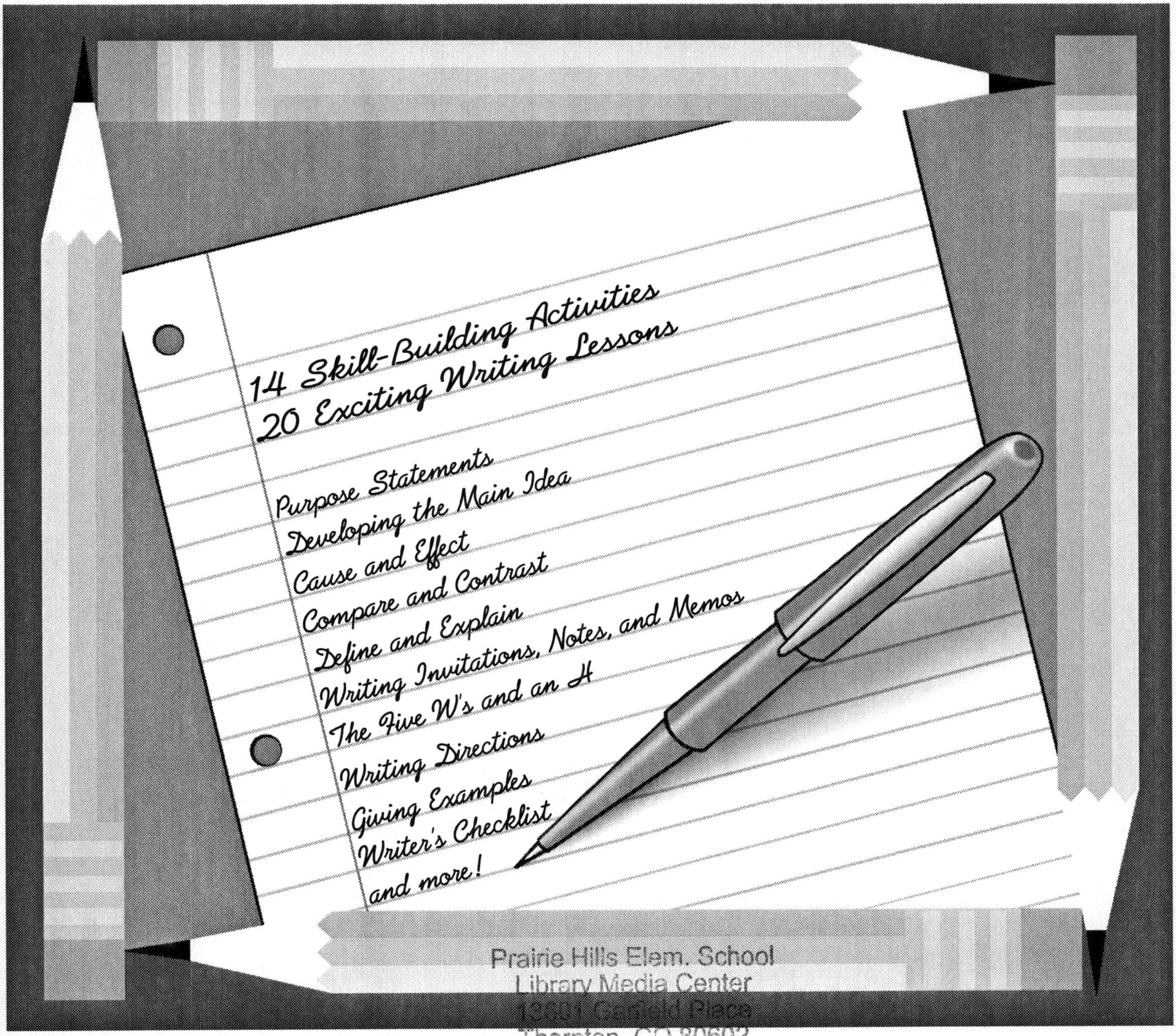

Written by Barbara Doherty and Charlotte Jaffe
Illustrated by Karen Birchak

ISBN 978-1-56644-099-8

Printed in the U.S.A.

Table of Contents

To the Teacher

It is important for children to develop excellent skills in expository writing. The first part of the book teaches about expository writing, reviews important composition skills, and provides opportunities for youngsters to practice those skills. Also included are a Writer's Checklist and an Editorial Symbols sheet.

The second part of the book comprises twenty writing lessons. By completing the easy-to-follow activities, students will quickly learn to write a variety of expository writings. Each two-page lesson is divided into three steps: Pre-Writing, Composing, and Revising. There is also a For-More-Fun activity for each lesson. It provides an opportunity for students to think creatively and to share their writing with their classmates and others. A list of additional topics for expository writing is also provided.

TEACHING TIPS

- Decide how long you would like each writing product to be and provide guidelines for your students before they begin each lesson.

- Expository (explanatory) writing must include a main idea, which should be fully developed. Spaces are provided encouraging students to brainstorm for a good main idea and to create lists of ideas, phrases, and words to develop into supporting detail sentences.

- Introduce some ways to develop the main idea: giving examples, using comparisons, describing the cause and effect, and defining and explaining.

- Allow enough time for students to write ideas in the Pre-writing section; instruct them to use short phrases for this step. In the Compose section, students will develop the phrases into longer, more fluent sentences.

- Discuss the use of key sequence words *(time order* and *space order)* when giving directions or providing an account of an event.

- Advise students to use the fewest words possible to accomplish their goal.

- In some activities, students are asked to write letters. Review the parts of a business letter and of a friendly letter with the students before the start of the writing activity.

- Encourage your students to work together in a positive way to revise their writing. Assign writing partners before beginning each writing activity. After using the Writer's Checklist, student writing partners can add personal comments. Some sample comments follow:

    This section of writing can be improved by adding or changing…
    What I liked about your expository writing is…

- Review the list of editorial symbols. Explain their use.

Review of Basic Composition Skills

SENTENCES:
A sentence is a group of words that expresses a complete thought. All sentences start with a capital letter and end with some form of punctuation.

Declarative Sentence: A declarative sentence makes a statement. It ends with a period.
EXAMPLE: I went sledding down a big hill.

Interrogative Sentence: An interrogative sentence asks a question. It ends with a question mark.
EXAMPLE: Will it rain tomorrow?

Exclamatory Sentence: An exclamatory sentence makes a forceful statement. It ends with an exclamation point.
EXAMPLE: Our team won the game!

Imperative Sentence: An imperative sentence gives a command. It ends with a period or an exclamation point.
EXAMPLE: Please bring me the book. Watch out!

Compound Sentences:
To make your writing more interesting, use sentences of different lengths. You can combine two short sentences into a compound sentence. A compound sentence contains two or more simple sentences that are joined by a conjunction. A comma is usually used before the conjunction in a compound sentence.
EXAMPLE: The dinner was delicious. I ate too much.
The dinner was delicious, but I ate too much.

TRANSITIONAL WORDS AND PHRASES:
Words that connect sentences or paragraphs are called transitional words. They include time-order words, space-order words, and words that help to clarify.

Time-Order Words: first, next, last
Space-Order Words: beneath, near, above
Words that Clarify: for instance, however, therefore

CAPITALIZATION RULES:
Capitalize the first word of every sentence.
Capitalize the names of holidays.
Capitalize proper nouns.
Capitalize the names of months and days.
Capitalize the pronoun *I*.
Capitalize the first word of a direct quotation.
Capitalize the first word in the greeting and closing of a letter.
Capitalize the first and every important word in a title.
Capitalize titles or abbreviations with a person's name.

Let's Explain

Expository writing informs the reader. The writer supplies information to help others understand something. This information may explain directions, how something works, an event, a natural occurrence, or an opinion. The writing may take many forms. Some of these are editorials, non-fiction stories, speeches, poetry, interpretation of literature, compositions, essays, research papers, dialogue, and newspaper or magazine articles. In any form, expository writing should be clear and easy to understand.

Many writing products may be classified in more than one way. For example, a travel brochure might be considered to be informative, or expository. It may also be considered an example of persuasive writing because an important purpose is to convince the reader to visit that particular place.

Read the following example of expository writing. Then answer the questions.

A fire in the apartment building located at Main and Oak streets last night was quickly brought under control by Engine Co. #5. The fire department was called into action at 11:30 p.m. in response to an automatic alarm. Upon arrival, firefighters quickly determined that all residents had been evacuated. Mr. James Smith, the building superintendent, credits the automatic alarm system with the safe evacuation of the residents and the limited damage to the building. The flames were confined to the front lower floor of the building. The blaze is under investigation.

1. What does the article explain?

____

____

____

____

____

2. What facts are supplied?

____

____

____

____

____

Getting off to a Good Start

A **purpose statement** acts as a guide for you, the writer. Putting down on paper what you want to explain will help you keep to the topic. The purpose statement keeps you focused throughout the process of writing about your topic. The following are two examples. Which do you think is the better one?

Very General: I will explain all about North America.
Gives More Focus: I will explain about the physical features of North America.

A **topic sentence** gives the main idea of the paragraph. It is often at the beginning of the paragraph. Add two sentences which give **details** to each of the topic sentences.

1. Our class will have a party.

____

____

2. My dog is very loyal.

____

____

A **headline** tells in a few words what the topic of an article is. It is written to attract the attention and the interest of the readers. Read the sample headlines. Write two questions for each.

Family Dog Saves the Day!

____

____

Trapped Girl Rescued

____

____

Historic Building Is Saved

____

____

To **hook** your reader, you must write something interesting. Your beginning should make your readers want to continue reading. Hooks can be written as a dialogue, a quotation, a question, or an exclamation. Below are examples of good beginning sentences. Write a short paragraph using one of them as a hook.

1. Imagine a world without television!
2. What would you do with a million dollars?
3. My mother knew the President.
4. "Give me liberty, or give me death," said Patrick Henry.

The Importance of Sequence

Explanations of how an event happened should be made in the correct **sequence,** or **order.** Certain words and phrases help clarify sequence. Some which clarify time order are *first, second, after, finally, to begin, next, then,* and *in conclusion.* Some which clarify space order are *left, right, above, beneath, east of,* and *west of.*

The sentences in the following paragraphs are out of order. Rewrite them in the correct sequence.

The Sandwich

As soon as the ingredients were assembled, I placed a slice of bread on the plate and spread mustard on it. Then I gathered the ingredients I'd need to make the sandwich and placed them near the plate and knife. I was hungry, so I decided to make a ham sandwich. Finally, I cleaned up the kitchen. It was delicious! Then I cut the sandwich into halves and ate it. After spreading the mustard, I added ham and lettuce and placed the other slice of bread on top. First I took out a plate and a knife and put them on the counter.

____

____

____

____

____

At the Zoo

Our third stop was the area where the lions roamed. Yesterday our class went to the zoo. After leaving the reptile house, we proceeded to the monkey house, where we enjoyed the animals' playful antics. We watched the lions and their cubs for a while and then strolled to the cafeteria, where we met the other groups for lunch. When we arrived, we separated into groups. Our guide told us many interesting and amusing facts about tortoises, snakes, and lizards. My group went to the reptile house first. It was a long ride, but we finally arrived back at school, tired but happy. After lunch we visited a few more animals and then headed for the parking lot, where our bus awaited us.

____

____

____

____

____

Writing Activity

On another piece of paper, write a paragraph with the sentences out of order. Exchange it with a classmate to rewrite.

Developing the Main Idea: Defining and Explaining

The main idea can be developed by defining the topic and explaining different aspects of it. Certain phrases and words are helpful in defining and explaining a topic. Some of these are *is made of, like, alike, the same as, different from, means, consists of, comprises, is/are, has/have, that,* and *as well as.*

EXAMPLE: What are mammals? Mammals are animals that give birth to live babies, are covered with hair, are warm-blooded, and have bodies which make food for the babies. Some mammals are elephants, dolphins, dogs, cats, and horses as well as humans.

Define the Topic

Write a definition of each of the following topics.

1. VOLCANOES

____

____

2. HARBORS

____

____

3. DECIDUOUS TREES

____

____

Writing Activity

Choose one of the above topics. Write a short paragraph in which you define the topic and then develop it by adding other sentences which explain it.

____

____

____

____

____

____

____

____

Developing the Main Idea: Using Cause and Effect

Explaining the relationship between **cause and effect** is one way to develop the main idea. Some words and phrases which help make this connection are *caused by, due to, if...then, as a result, therefore, so, because,* and *brought about.*

EXAMPLE: **Because** I was practicing every day, there was an improvement in my soccer skills. The **cause** is the daily practice. The **effect** is the improvement in soccer skills. *Because* is a transitional word. It helps connect the cause and the effect.

Main Idea: Clocks and watches are helpful.
Detail sentence: Because I had my watch, I got to the appointment on time.
Detail sentence: I am not late for school because my alarm clock wakes me.
Detail sentence: Ahmad lost his watch; as a result, he was late for everything.

Complete Them

Complete the following cause-and-effect sentences. Add punctuation as needed.

1. Because it rained ______________________________
2. We were late for the party because ______________________________
3. Due to the flat tire ______________________________
4. ______________________________ as a result of doing all my chores.
5. Because I studied for the test ______________________________

Figure It Out!

Read the following paragraph. Find the main idea and the cause-and-effect relationships.

Deer are becoming garden pests, often invading home yards, garden, and parks. The principal reason is the loss of their woodland habitat caused by increased development. Due to this loss of habitat, deer and other animals must look for food in new places. People are becoming upset because of the damage done by the deer.

Main Idea: ______________________________

Cause: ____________________ Effect: ____________________

Cause: ____________________ Effect: ____________________

Cause: ____________________ Effect: ____________________

Writing Activity

On another paper, develop one of these topics into a short paragraph: a pet, smoking, landfills, or school dress codes. Use cause and effect to create the detail sentences to develop your main idea.

Developing the Main Idea: Using Comparison

When developing a topic, it is often helpful to use comparison and contrast to explain your ideas clearly. ***Compare*** may focus on likenesses alone or on likenesses and differences. ***Contrast*** always emphasizes differences. Some words and phrases that help us make comparisons are *both, on the other hand, unlike, but, in the same way, similar, different,* and *also.*

EXAMPLE: Cars and buses are alike because they both have wheels. They are both used as transportation. They have many similar parts. Buses are usually larger than even the largest cars. Buses can carry more passengers.

Compare and Contrast

TIGERS AND LIONS...

are alike because ____

are unlike because ____

COWS AND HORSES...

are alike because ____

are unlike because ____

ROSES AND TULIPS...

are alike because ____

are unlike because ____

CLOCKS AND CALENDARS...

are alike because ____

are unlike because ____

Writing Activities

Write a short paragraph comparing of one of these pairs: apples and oranges, dogs and cats, baseball and basketball, or frogs and toads.

____

____

____

____

____

____

____

Developing the Main Idea: Using Examples

An effective way to develop a main idea is by description and examples. Each supporting detail sentence can be an example of the statement you are making in your main-idea sentence. The following words and phrases are especially helpful when you are giving examples: *one way, another way, another kind, for instance, also, in addition,* and *as an example.*

EXAMPLE:

Dogs are very helpful to humans. One example is the seeing-eye dog. Seeing-eye dogs are trained to help blind people. Some dogs are trained to help police officers. Others are used to search for bombs if there is a bomb scare and for drugs in airports and other locations. In addition, there are special dogs trained to find people lost in earthquakes, avalanches, and other disasters.

Write an Example

Write a detail sentence for each of these main ideas by giving an example.

1. Whales are very large animals.

____

2. Some snakes are very dangerous.

____

3. Going to the beach can be lots of fun.

____

4. There are many resources in libraries in addition to books.

____

Writing Activity

Choose one of the above main ideas. Write a paragraph in which you develop that main idea by giving examples.

____

____

____

____

____

____

____

____

Writing How-to Directions

When giving directions for making or doing something, you must be very clear. Follow these guidelines when giving directions:

1. State your purpose.
2. Give directions in sequence.
3. Keep your sentences short.
4. Do not include any unnecessary information.
5. If possible, provide a drawing or a diagram to help clarify your written directions.
6. Check your directions by reviewing them from the readers' point of view.

How To…

Choose one of the following and write directions explaining how to do it.

HOW TO MAKE PANCAKES
HOW TO BUILD A BIRDHOUSE
HOW TO GIVE YOUR DOG A BATH
HOW TO MAKE FUDGE
HOW TO BUILD A BIRDHOUSE
HOW TO MAKE HOMEMADE PIZZA
HOW TO BUILD A MODEL CAR

HOW TO…

____

____

____

____

____

____

____

____

____

____

____

____

____

Create a chart or other visual aid to go along with your how-to directions.

Writing Directions to a Place

When you give directions from one place to another, you must be sure that they are clear and easy to understand. Include permanent landmarks as reference points. Use sequence words and direction words. You will also want to include distance as part of your directions. Keep your sentences short and uncomplicated. Check yourself to make sure that your directions will be clear to your readers.

EXAMPLES OF SEQUENCE, DIRECTION, AND DISTANCE WORDS:

Sequence Words: *first, next, then, last, finally,* and *begin*

Direction Words: *north, east, south, west, left, right*

Distance Words: *miles, blocks, feet*

EXAMPLE:

Begin at the public library and walk **north** on Main Street for **three blocks. Then** turn **right** onto Bridge Street. Stay on Bridge Street for **two blocks. Next,** turn **right** onto River Road. My house is the **third** house on the **left**. It is the grey one with white shutters. The house number is 227.

Give Directions

Pretend that you are having a pool party for your baseball team. Not everyone coming knows where you live. Write directions from the school to your house.

____

____

____

____

____

____

____

____

____

____

____

____

____

____

Create a map to go along with your directions.

Writing a News Article Using the Five W's and an H

A news article tells about an event that has happened. The article reports the facts of the event, not opinions. There are five basic questions that should be answered in the article: **Who** was involved in the event? **What** occurred? **When** did it happen? **Where** did it take place? **Why** did it happen? Sometimes a sixth question must also be included: **How** did it happen? The answers to these questions should be explained in the first paragraph.

Who? What? Where? When? Why? and *How?*

Read the following news article.

Brigantine, NJ The clam boat *Marie Elena* ran aground last night during a violent storm. High seas swamped the boat. The engine room was quickly flooded. The pumps couldn't keep up with the pounding surf and wind-driven waves. The coast guard responded to the distress call, bringing high-powered pumps. After several hours, the decision was made to abandon the boat. Captain Bob Burroughs and his crew were airlifted to the nearby U.S.C.G. base. All were reported to be in good condition. The salvage company S.O.S. will assess the situation today.

Now answer the questions about the article you just read.

WHO? ____________________

WHAT? ____________________

WHEN? ____________________

WHERE? ____________________

WHY? ____________________

HOW? ____________________

Write a news article of your own. Start by planning the five W's and an H of your article. For topics consider something that happened in your school or town.

____

____

____

____

____

____

____

____

____

Writing an Invitation

Invitations come in a variety of styles. They can be formal or informal, depending on the occasion. It is necessary to include the who, what, where, when, and why information that the receiver of the invitation must know in order to respond correctly.

Sometimes it is fun to plan a party with a theme. If you are honoring someone who has a particular interest or hobby, it may add to the enjoyment of the party if it is planned around that theme.

Fill in the Blanks

Fill in the blanks with the who, what, where, when, and why information to plan an invitation for a party you are hosting. Think of a theme and decorate your invitation accordingly.

JOIN THE FUN!

Come to a party for ____________________

on ________________________

from __________ to __________.

It will be held at

________________________________.

We are celebrating

________________________________.

R.S.V.P.____________________ at__________

Create an invitation to be used to invite others to a school activity. Use the space below to plan your who, what, where, when, and why information. Create your decorated invitation on another sheet of paper.

WHO? ____

WHAT? ____

WHEN? ____

WHERE? ____

WHY? ____

Writing Announcements and Notices

An announcement should begin with the topic. Each following item is an explanation of one of the details. Remember that announcements are not written to any one person. Be sure that it is clear to your entire audience.

EXAMPLE: The following is an example of an announcement about soccer sign-ups.

SOCCER SIGN-UPS

Registration for township soccer teams will be held for boys and girls ages six through thirteen from September 8 through September 24. Please note the locations and times:

Roberts School: Every evening from 5:00 p.m. to 8:00 p.m.
Township Community Center: Mondays and Wednesdays from 9:00 a.m. to 5:00 p.m.
Public Library: Saturdays from 9:00 a.m. to noon.

You must bring proof of age and residency. NO exceptions will be made!

Write an Announcement

Write a notice or announcement for an upcoming school play, art show, or other school or community event. Remember to include *all* the necessary information!

Writing Memos

A short message is called a **memorandum**, or memo for short. Messages should always be clear and purposeful—without any extra information. The date should always be included on the message. Memos are often used at school, at home, and at work. Do you remember any memos that have been sent to you or that you have sent to others? What memos might you want to write in the future?

EXAMPLE: The following is an example of a memo.

> DATE: January 25, 2002 TIME: 10:00 a.m.
>
> TO: Andrew Roberts
> FROM: Mrs. Stevens, Student Advisory Office
>
> MESSAGE: You have been assigned a new locker. It is available immediately. Please see Mr. Daniels in the office for your locker number and to get the combination.

Write Memos

Pretend you are Jami Patel, the captain of the safety patrol. Write a message to all patrol members advising them of the next meeting. Include the necessary who, what, when, where, why, and the how information in your message.

____

____

____

____

____

____

Write a memo of your own to a friend, teacher, or family member. Remember to include all important information.

____

____

____

____

____

____

Expository Writing Across the Curriculum

Expository writing is probably used by students more than any other kind of writing. You use it when you write a report on the Civil War for your social studies class or when you write a book report for your English class. You use expository writing when you write a lab report in your science class or when you explain why you chose a certain rule in math class. Perhaps you have been asked to explain the differences in the style of two artists in art class; you would have used expository writing then, too.

Examples of Writing in the Subject Areas

For each subject area, think of an assignment that would call for expository writing. Be specific. You may use actual assignments that you have been given or you may create your own.

EXAMPLE:
SOCIAL STUDIES—Write a report on the causes and events leading to the American Civil War.

GEOGRAPHY

____

____

____

SOCIAL STUDIES

____

____

____

SCIENCE

____

____

____

MATH

____

____

____

ENGLISH / LANGUAGE ARTS

____

____

____

Outline for an Expository Report

As preparation for writing a report or an essay, it is helpful to organize your information by using an outline. It may be a topic outline, as shown below, or it may be a sentence outline, in which complete sentences are used.

BASIC RULES FOR USING AN OUTLINE

1. Indent each number or letter and follow it with a period.
2. Capitalize the beginning of each entry.
3. Make your entries specific and clear.
4. Use Roman numerals for your main topics.
5. Use capital letters for your sub-topics.
6. Use cardinal numbers (1, 2, 3, etc.) for details.
7. Use lower case letters for more specific details.
8. If there is no "II," do not use "I." If there is no "B," do not use "A," etc.

SAMPLE TOPIC OUTLINE:

TREES OF NORTH AMERICA

I. Types of Trees (First Main Idea)
  A. Conifers (Supporting Facts)
    1. Definition
    2. Examples
      a. Firs
      b. Pines
      c. Spruce
  B. Deciduous (Supporting Facts)
    1. Definition
    2. Examples
      a. Maples
      b. Oaks
      c. Birches
II. Products from Trees (Second Main Idea)
  A. Foods (Supporting Facts)
  B. Medicines (Supporting Facts)
  C. Other products (Supporting Facts)
III. Conclusion

Outlining Practice

Suppose you were to write a report on baseball. Organize the following topics and sub-topics into the form of an outline.

Before 1950	American League	Night Baseball
All-Star Break	World War II	National League
After 1950	World Series	Introduction
Conclusion	Statistics	Hall of Fame

Writer's Checklist

This checklist provides some useful guidelines to remember when you write. Use it both for self-evaluation and for evaluation of your peers.

___ 1. Did you compose a good opening sentence that will catch the attention of the reader?

___ 2. Do you have a single focus in your writing? Did you stick to one topic?

___ 3. Is your writing organized? Does it progress logically from beginning to end? Is it clearly written and easy to follow?

___ 4. Did you use details in your writing that clarify and support the main topic?

___ 5. If you are writing non-fiction, did you make sure your writing is accurate?

___ 6. Did you check your work for spelling, punctuation, and grammar errors?

___ 7. Did you use sentence variety in your writing? Are your sentences of varied lengths? Did you start your sentences with different words?

___ 8. Did you use word variety in your writing? Check to see that you did not use the same word over and over.

___ 9. Did you use vivid vocabulary in your writing? Are your words interesting and colorful?

___ 10. If you used figures of speech, were they appropriate?

___ 11. Did you try the use of transitional words and phrases between paragraphs to make your writing easier to follow and understand?

___ 12. Did you use a good closing sentence? Does it sum up your writing in an effective way?

___ 13. Did you check your first draft carefully before attempting to revise and rewrite your work?

___ 14. Did you type your work or write it in a legible manner? Will people be able to read your work easily?

Writing Partner's Personal Comments:

____

____

____

____

____

Editorial Symbols

The following editorial symbols are some common symbols used in proofreading and editing. A caret or a line is used within the text to show where the correction should be made. A circle around instructions in the margin means not to include what's circled in the text.

IN MARGIN	MEANING	IN TEXT
ℒ	delete or take out	Take it ~~it~~ out.
⁀	close up; no space	The book is in the book bag.
father	replace	Joe visited his ~~mother~~.
#	insert space	Shewent to the store.
a	insert a letter, punctuation, or word	Anne, give the tall man book.
(ital)	set in italics	I just read Little Women.
(bf)	set in bold	Editorial Marks
(cap)	capitalize	joan and I went to the movies.
(lc)	lower case	The River was very high.
⊙	insert period	I asked her to come
^,	insert comma	She had a book a poster, and a magazine.
^;	insert semicolon	I went to the class so did Sue.
“ / ”	insert quotation marks	Go to bed, said Mrs. Jones.
’	insert apostrophe	Id like to go now.
(tr)	transpose words	The boy tall can reach the high shelf.
(tr)	transpose lines	Bring it here. Find the box.
¶	make new paragraph	¶ Dogs are very useful to humans. They have been trained as hunters. Some are used for security. Others are work animals, pulling carts and sleds. Many dogs help people with handicaps maintain their independence. Dogs are very good companions.
no ¶	no new paragraph	Dogs are very useful to humans. They have been trained as hunters. Some are used for security. Others are work animals, pulling carts and sleds. Many dogs help people with handicaps maintain their independence. Dogs are very good companions.

All-Star Camp

TOPIC

Even if you have not attended one, you probably know about sports camps. Some of these are day camps. Others are overnight camps; campers live at these camps for one or more weeks. Create a flyer telling about registration for a camp featuring a particular sport or sports in general.

THINK ABOUT IT

Remember to include the five W's and an H. What is the name of the camp? Where is it? When will the camp be in session? Who should attend? Why should they attend? Which sport or sports will be featured? Who will the instructors/counselors be? What skills will be taught? How will they be taught? What other kinds of activities will be included? What is the cost? How does one register? Who should be contacted for information?

GET ORGANIZED

Plan your flyer. A clear opening sentence will help capture your readers' interest. Fill in the who, what, where, when, why, and how information to help you develop your ideas. Use words, phrases, and/or short sentences. You can develop your writing into more complete, fluent sentences in the Compose section.

Heading: ______________________________

Opening Sentence: ______________________________

____

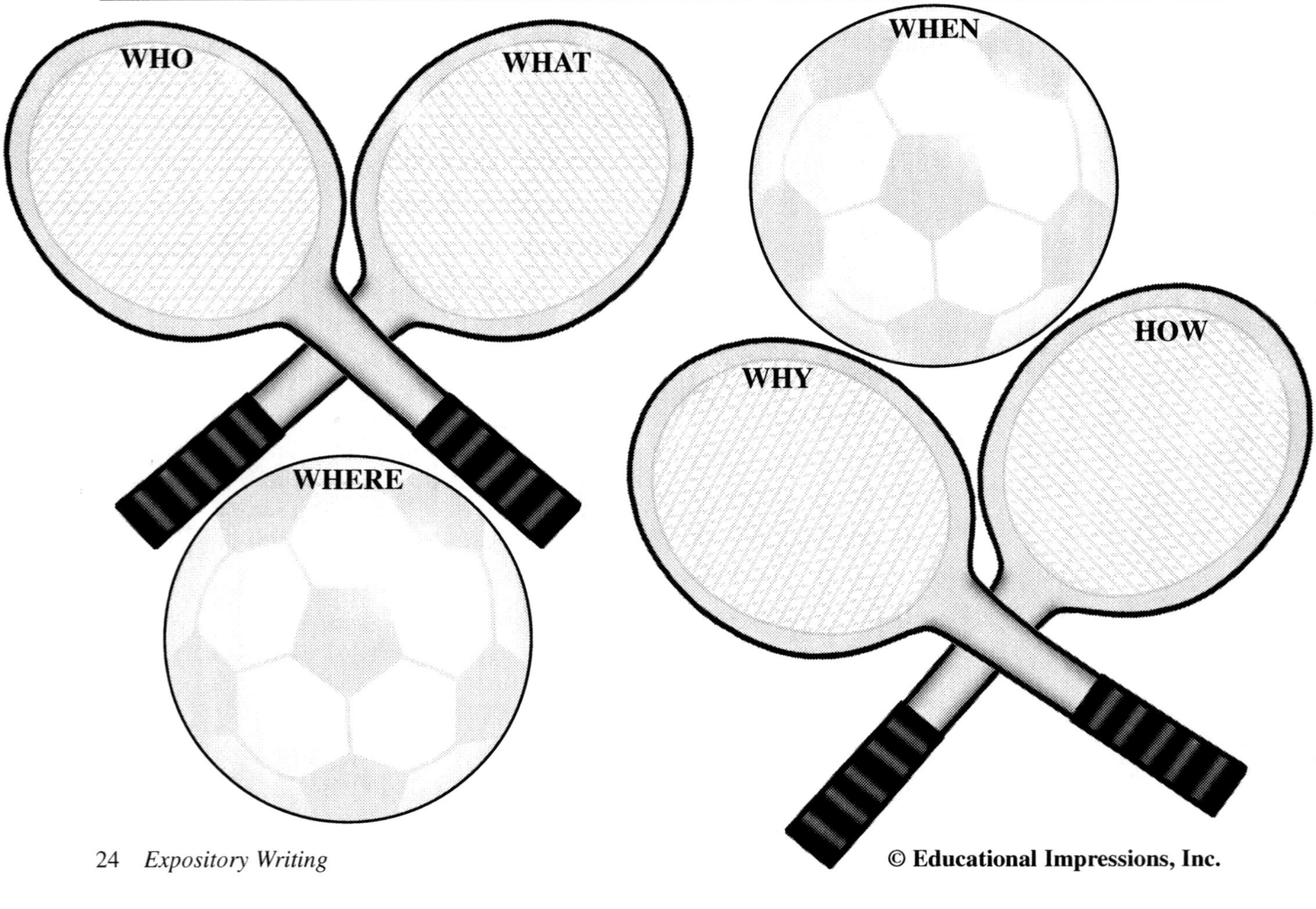

All-Star Camp

COMPOSE

Each paragraph in your flyer should have a clearly stated main idea and at least three sentences with facts to support it. Think about the various ways to develop your writing: examples, comparison, definition and explanation, and cause and effect. Decide which is best for this writing. Remember to include the necessary who, what, when, where, why, and how information in your expository writing. Refer to your writing ideas from the pre-writing section to get started.

REVISE

Edit your writing by using the Writer's Checklist and the Editorial Symbols sheets. Then exchange papers with your pre-assigned writing partner. Each of you will use the same sheets to offer suggestions for improvement to the other. Now you are ready to rewrite your work in good form on another paper. Share the flyer with the whole class.

FOR-MORE-FUN ACTIVITY

Create a table display for the sport or sports featured in your brochure. Include posters, equipment, uniforms, score cards, and other appropriate items.

A Craft-and-Flower Show

TOPIC

Your class sponsored a combined craft-and-flower show as a fund raiser for a local charity. Write an article for your school newspaper describing the event.

THINK ABOUT IT

Who was in charge? Who came? When was it held? Where was it held? Why was it held? Were there any especially interesting items? Were things on exhibit? Where things for sale? Was it the first time your class organized a craft-and-flower show? Was it the first time it held a fund raiser? What planning was involved? How was it advertised? What were the results of the event?

GET ORGANIZED

Plan your article. Decide upon a good headline. Write a clear opening sentence to help capture your readers' interest. Fill in the who, what, where, when, why, and how information to help you develop your ideas. Use words, phrases, and/or short sentences. You can develop your writing into more complete, fluent sentences in the Compose section.

Heading: ________________________________

Opening Sentence: ________________________________

____

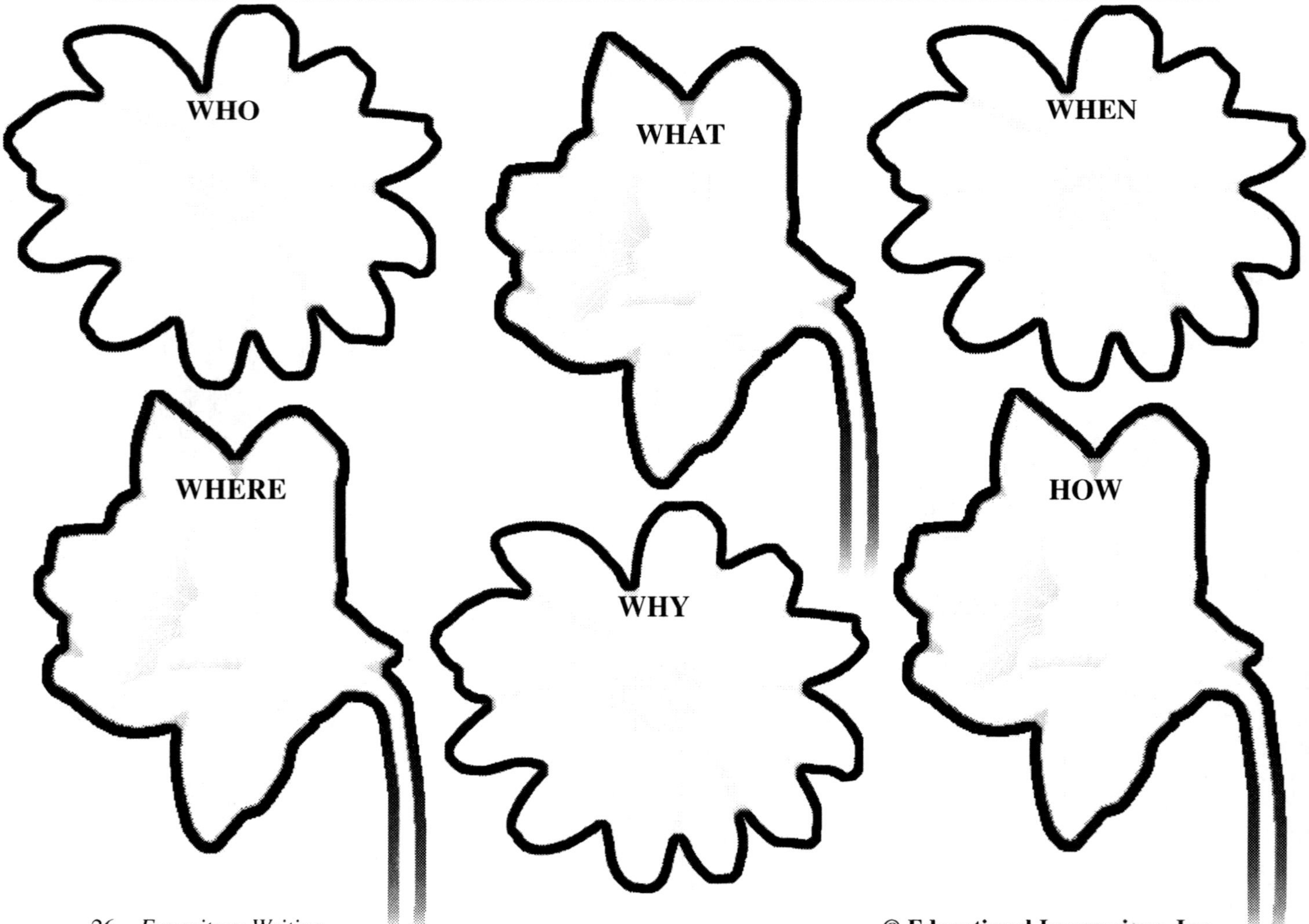

A Craft-and-Flower Show

COMPOSE

Begin by choosing a headline that serves to tell readers what the topic will be. Each paragraph in your article should have a clearly stated main idea and at least three sentences with facts to support it. Think about the various ways to develop your writing: examples, comparison, definition and explanation, and cause and effect. Decide which is best for this writing. Remember to include the necessary who, what, when, where, why, and how information in your expository writing. Refer to your writing ideas from the pre-writing section to get started.

REVISE

Edit your article by using the Writer's Checklist and the Editorial Symbols sheets. Then exchange papers with your pre-assigned writing partner. Each of you will use the same sheets to offer suggestions for improvement to the other. Now you are ready to rewrite your work in good form on another paper. Share the article with the whole class.

FOR MORE FUN

Design the award that is given to the first-place winner at the show.

How to Play Checkers

TOPIC

You have been asked to entertain your younger cousin, who wants to learn how to play checkers. You like this cousin and are happy to teach her. Once she learns how to play, it will be fun for you, too. Put your directions on a poster so that your cousin can refer to them from time to time.

THINK ABOUT IT

Put yourself in your cousin's place. Be encouraging! Start by explaining the object of the game. Continue with directions on how to set up the board. You will have to explain the rules of the game. Don't forget to include helpful strategies that you have learned. Help your cousin to become competitive with you so that you will enjoy playing against her. Some people learn by reading about something. Others learn by doing.

GET ORGANIZED

Plan your directions. Begin by explaining your purpose and the object of the game. Explain the rules of the game and helpful strategies by using words, phrases, and/or short sentences. You can develop your writing into more complete, fluent sentences in the Compose section.

Purpose Statement: ____

Definition and Object of the Game: ________________________________

____

____

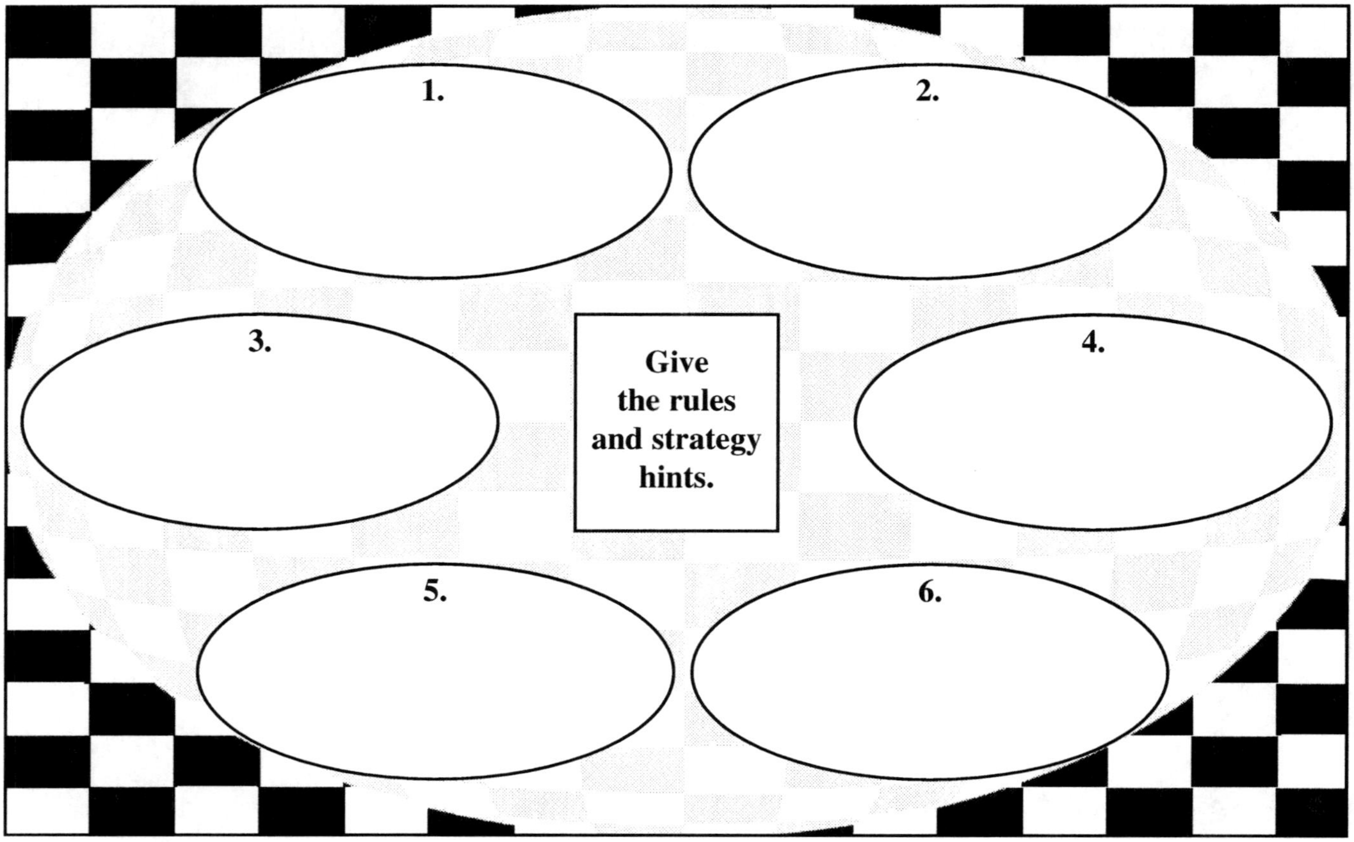

How to Play Checkers

COMPOSE

Begin by stating the purpose of your expository writing. You will use definition and explanation to develop your writing. Keep your sentences short and be sure to keep your directions in the proper sequence. Use words like *first, next, last,* and *finally* to help you. Do not include any unnecessary information. Assume your reader knows nothing about checkers! Refer to your writing ideas from the pre-writing section to get started. Check your directions by reviewing them from the reader's point of view. If possible, provide a drawing or a diagram to help clarify your written directions.

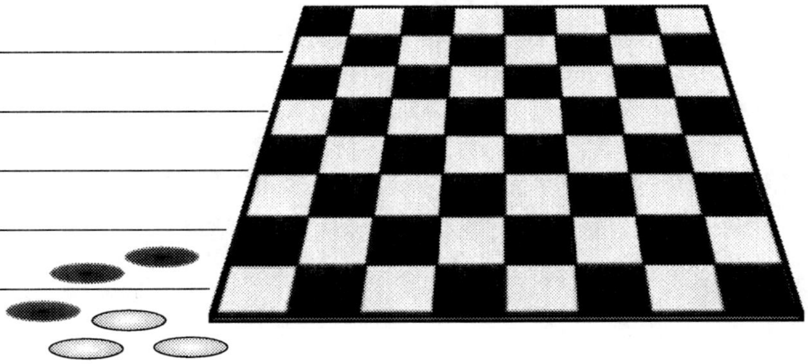

REVISE

Edit your writing by using the Writer's Checklist and the Editorial Symbols sheets. Then exchange papers with your pre-assigned writing partner. Each of you will use the same sheets to offer suggestions for improvement to the other. Now you are ready to rewrite your work in good form on another paper. Put your directions on a sheet of oaktag or construction paper. You may want to include a drawing or diagram. Share the poster with the whole class.

FOR MORE FUN

Make a word-search puzzle using words containing "check" or vocabulary about checkers and the rules of the game.

Man's Best Friend

TOPIC

Dogs have been called "man's best friend" for a very long time. Your assignment for English class is to write a paragraph explaining why people feel this way. Entitle your paragraph "Man's Best Friend." (It does not matter whether or not you agree with the premise.)

THINK ABOUT IT

Dogs are used for companionship. In what other ways are they used? How are they trained? Whom do they help? Have you read or heard in the news about dogs helping people? Can you think of any instances in which a dog acted heroically?

GET ORGANIZED

Plan your expository writing. Begin by writing an opening statement. It will act as a guide for you. Use words, phrases, and/or short sentences. You can develop your writing into more complete, fluent sentences in the Compose section.

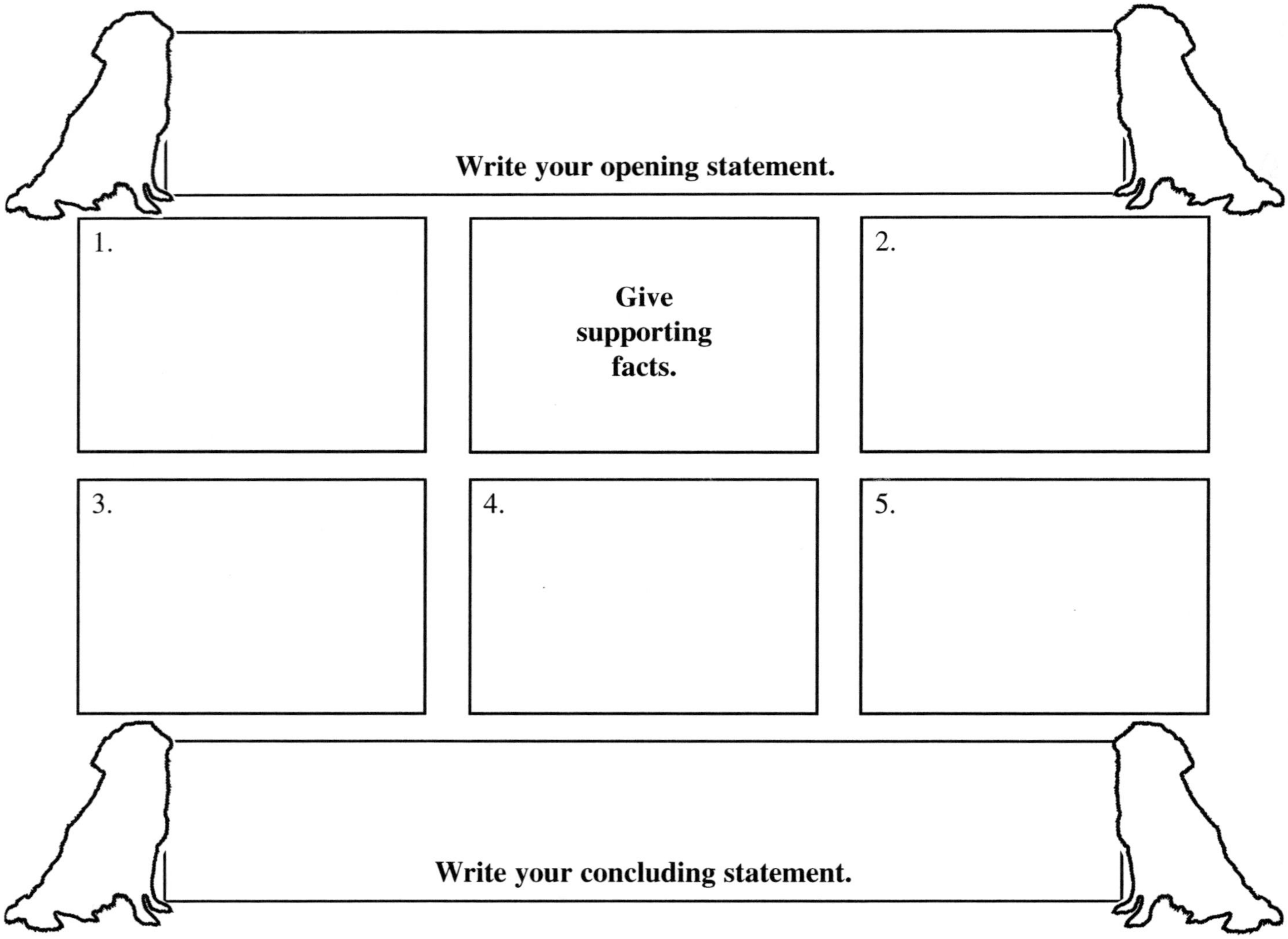

Man's Best Friend

COMPOSE

Your paragraph will explain why dogs are often called "Man's Best Friend." Use a topic sentence to state your main idea. Develop that idea by explaining different aspects of it and giving examples of each. Be sure to keep to the topic. Restate your main idea in your concluding sentence. Refer to your writing ideas from the pre-writing section to get started.

REVISE

Edit your expository writing by using the Writer's Checklist and the Editorial Symbols sheets. Then exchange papers with your pre-assigned writing partner. Each of you will use the same sheets to offer suggestions for improvement to the other. Now you are ready to rewrite your work in good form on another paper. Share your writing with the whole class.

FOR MORE FUN

Design an award for a "hero" dog. Some possibilities are a trophy, a plaque, and a collar. Write a paragraph explaining the award. Include the 5 W's.

My Favorite Family Activity

TOPIC

The local parent-teacher organization in your town sponsors activities to encourage family togetherness and is in the process of assembling a catalog of events and ideas. The organization has asked for suggestions from the students in your school. You are to write a paragraph about your favorite family activity.

THINK ABOUT IT

Make a list of activities you have enjoyed with your family: family celebrations, vacations, visits to museums, sports activities and events, spectator activities, building something together, accomplishing a job together, and other activities. Which is your favorite? Is your favorite activity one that you do regularly? If so, how often? Is it a simple activity, such as preparing a Saturday breakfast together, or is it something more involved? Which family members are involved? Do you have a special role in this activity?

GET ORGANIZED

Plan your expository writing. Begin by writing an opening statement. It will act as a guide for you. Use words, phrases, and/or short sentences. You can develop your writing into more complete, fluent sentences in the Compose section.

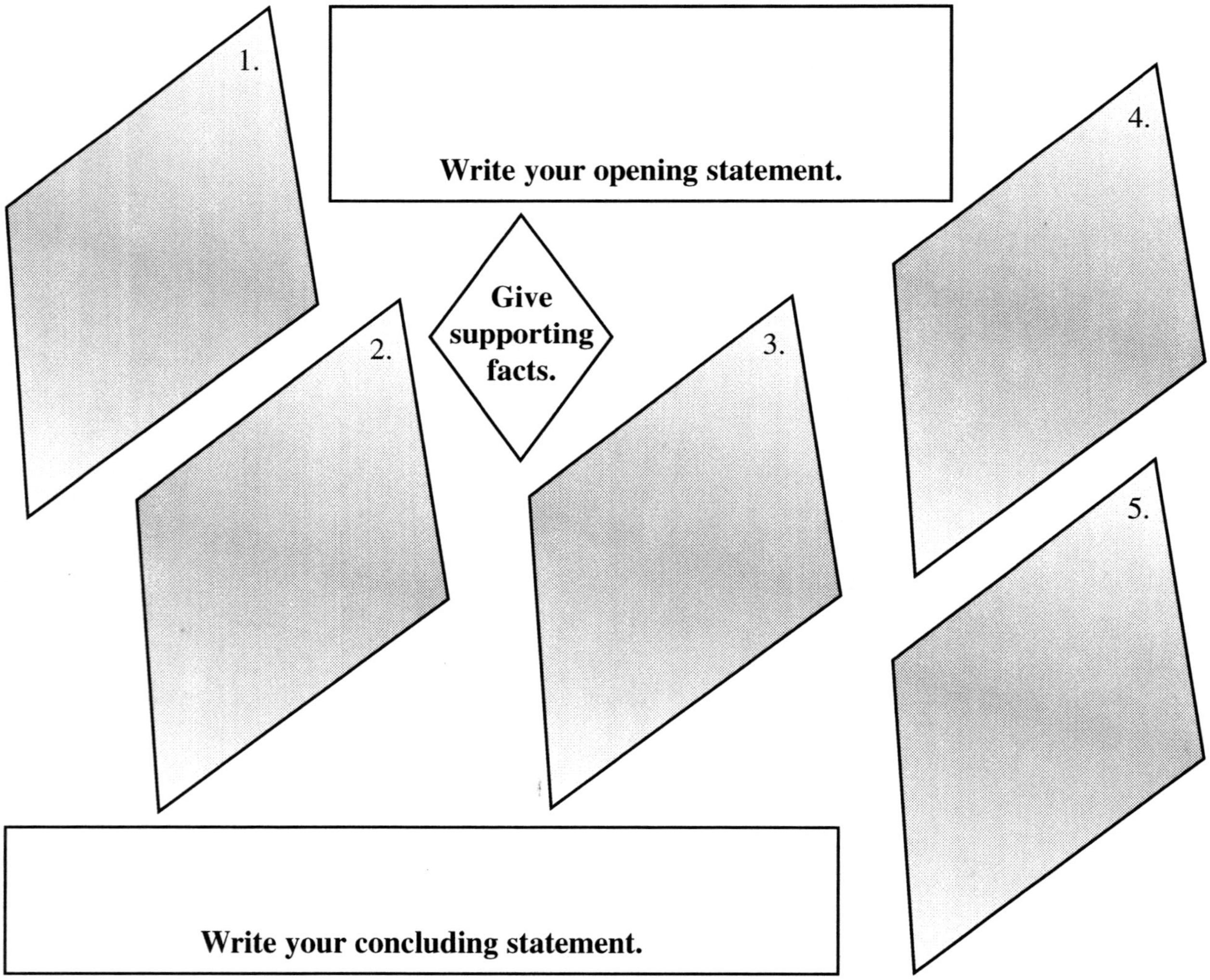

My Favorite Family Activity

COMPOSE

Your paragraph will explain a favorite family activity. Use a topic sentence to state your main idea. Develop that idea by explaining different aspects of it and giving examples of each. Be sure to keep to the topic and to present your facts in their proper order. Restate your main idea in your concluding sentence. Refer to your writing ideas from the pre-writing section to get started.

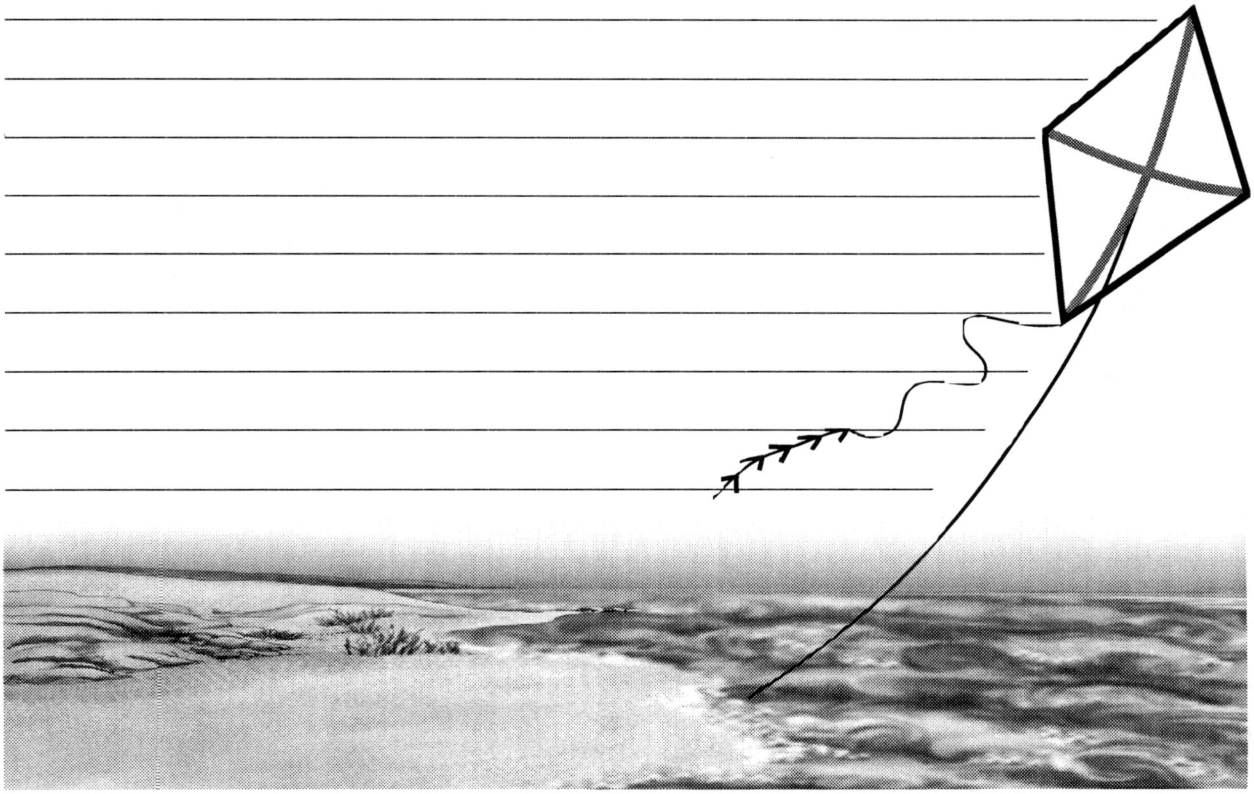

REVISE

Edit your paragraph by using the Writer's Checklist and the Editorial Symbols sheets. Then exchange papers with your pre-assigned writing partner. Each of you will use the same sheets to offer suggestions for improvement to the other. Now you are ready to rewrite your work in good form on another paper. Share your writing with the whole class.

FOR MORE FUN

Create a greeting card telling your family how much you enjoy doing things together. Include an appropriate illustration.

School Game Night

TOPIC

You are on the committee to plan a School Game Night. Students and their families will gather for a fun-filled evening of participating in a variety of board games. Students will be asked to bring a few of their favorite games. Your job is to prepare the notice explaining the event.

THINK ABOUT IT

What information should you include? Where will the activity take place? When will it take place? Who should attend? Why should they attend? What type of games will be featured? Who will be in charge? Will other kinds of activities be included? Will refreshments be served? Who will provide them? Is there any cost? Are volunteer helpers needed? How do you register? How do you get more information?

GET ORGANIZED

Plan your notice. A clear opening sentence will help capture your readers' interest. Fill in the who, what, where, when, why, and how information to help you develop your ideas. Use words, phrases, and/or short sentences. You can develop your writing into more complete, fluent sentences in the Compose section.

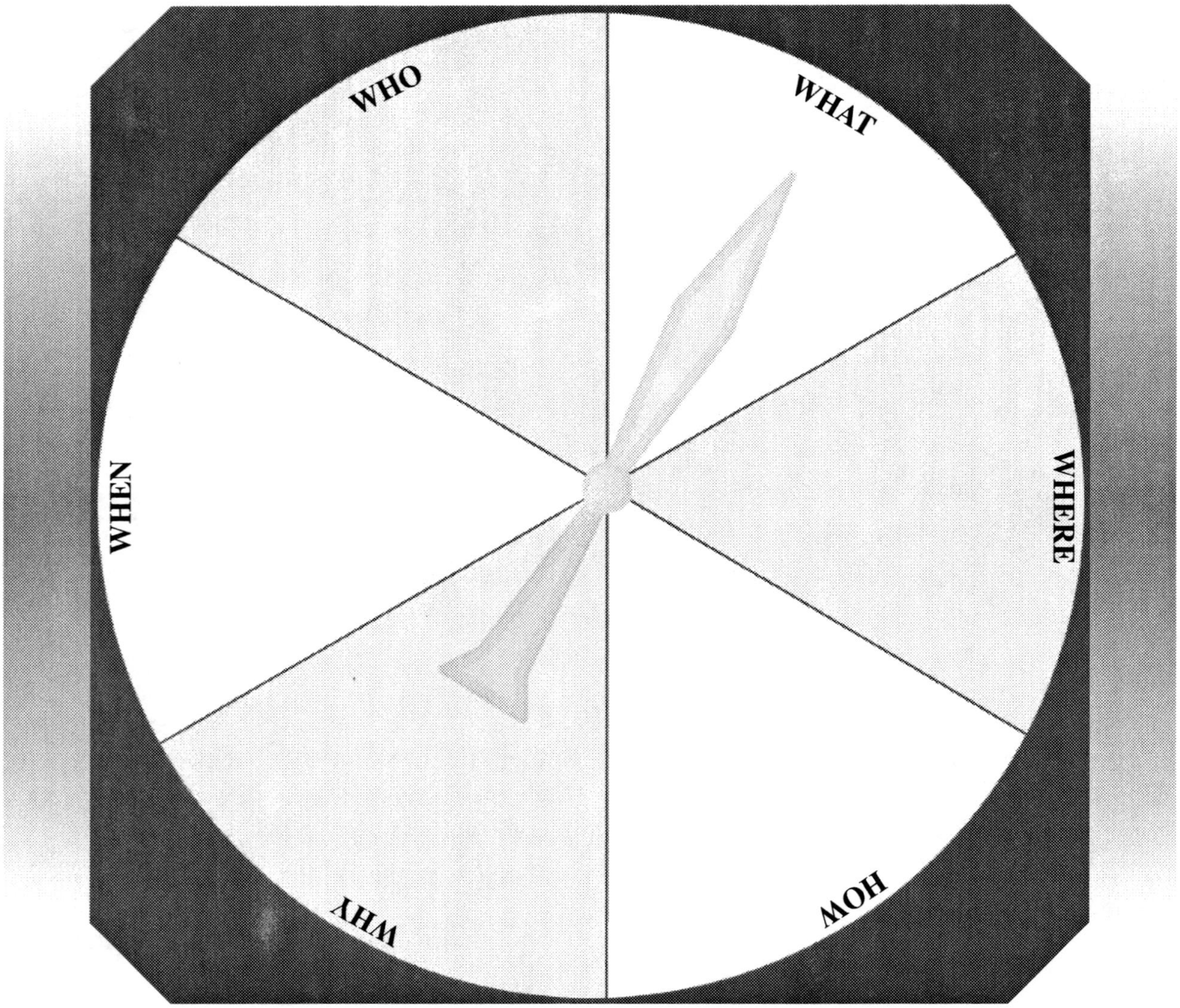

School Game Night

COMPOSE

Clearly explain the reason for the notice. Remember to include the necessary who, what, when, where, why, and how information in your expository writing. Refer to your writing ideas from the pre-writing section to get started.

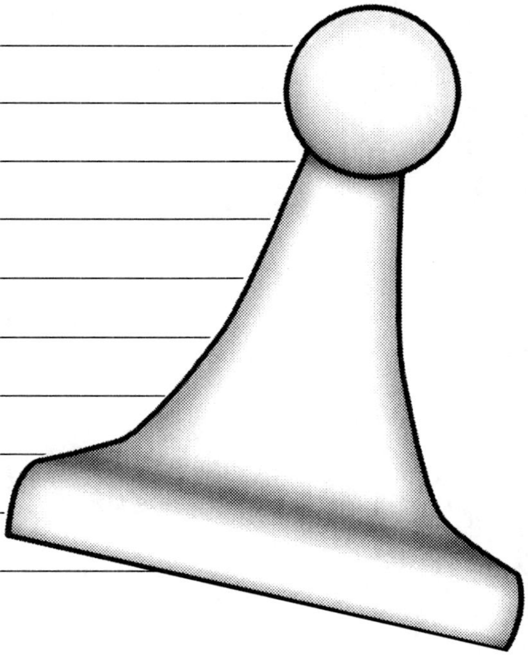

REVISE

Edit your notice by using the Writer's Checklist and the Editorial Symbols sheets. Then exchange papers with your pre-assigned writing partner. Each of you will use the same sheets to offer suggestions for improvement to the other. Now you are ready to rewrite your work in good form on another paper. Share the notice with the whole class.

FOR MORE FUN

Take a survey in your school. How many think a School Game Night would be a good idea for your school?

Morning Announcements

TOPIC

Morning announcements at your school bring you much useful information. Some of the items are reminders of past announcements. Others explain new or temporary schedules. There may be an explanation of a certain holiday. Contests, competitions, and other events may be explained. Choose a few topics and write a script for the morning announcements at your school.

THINK ABOUT IT

What types of announcements will you include? You might announce a special event, such as an assembly, a class trip, or an athletic event. Perhaps you will tell about changes in scheduling for transportation, club meetings, team practice, after-school programs, or other events. Think about the 5 W's and an H when you are planning your announcement script.

GET ORGANIZED

Plan your expository writing. An announcement should begin with the topic. Use the boxes to record information about the events you will announce. Include necessary who, what, when, where, why, and how information for each. Use words, phrases, and/or short sentences. You can develop your writing into more complete, fluent sentences in the Compose section.

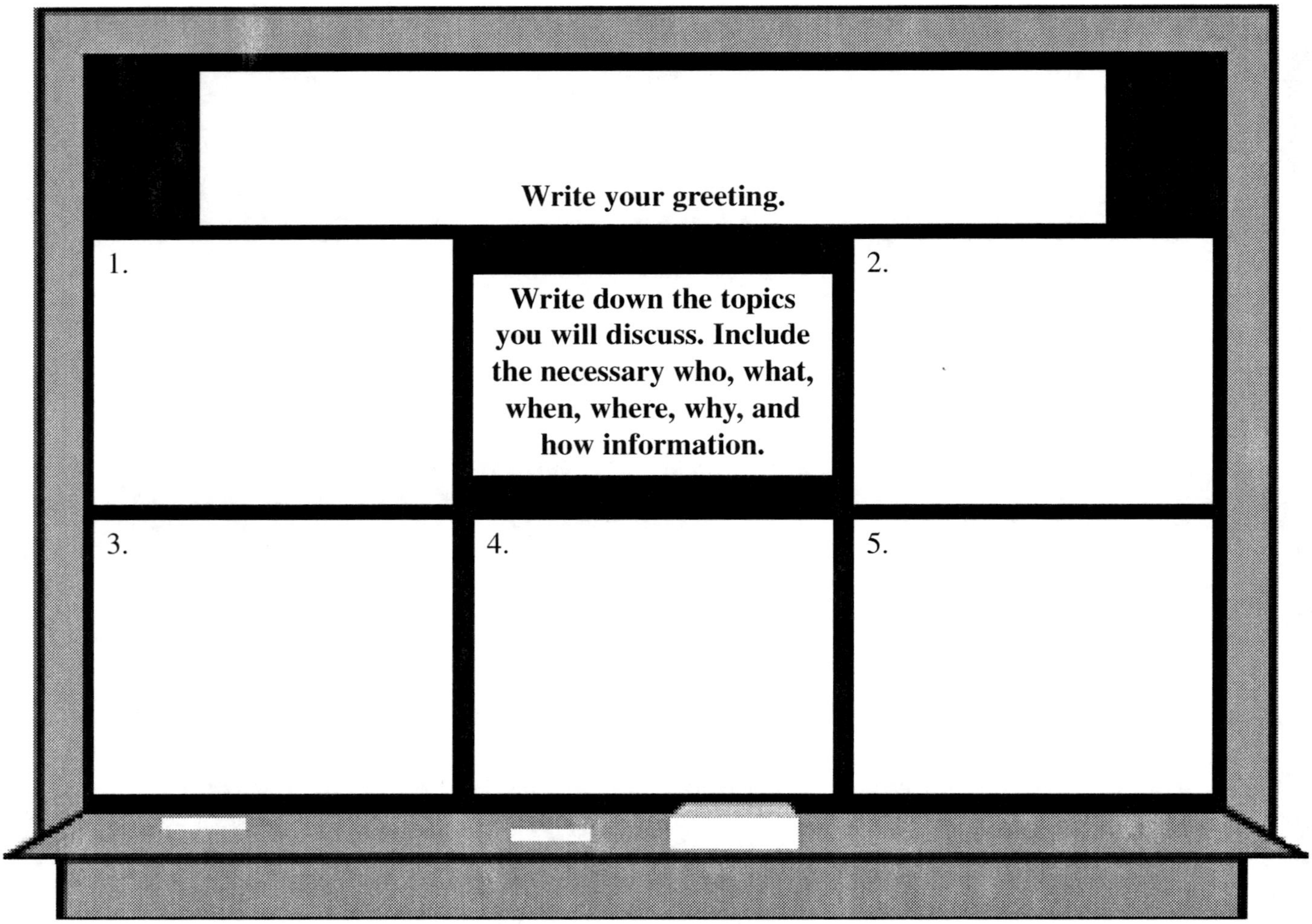

Morning Announcements

COMPOSE

Your expository writing will be in the form of an announcement to be read over the school PA system. Begin by clearly describing the main idea of your announcement. Follow with sentences that tell who, what, when, where, why, and how details. Repeat the process for every item you wish to include in the announcement. Refer to your writing ideas from the pre-writing section to get started.

REVISE

Edit your expository writing by using the Writer's Checklist and the Editorial Symbols sheets. Then exchange papers with your pre-assigned writing partner. Each of you will use the same sheets to offer suggestions for improvement to the other. Now you are ready to rewrite your work in good form on another paper. Share the announcement with the whole class.

FOR MORE FUN

Record yourself reading the morning announcement you have written. Play it for your class.

A Literary Wax Museum

TOPIC

After reading many popular novels, your class has created a wax museum exhibit to share the main characters of these stories with others. Everyone is excited about the reading they have done and the idea of sharing what they've learned. Write an invitation to be sent to those you'd like to attend.

THINK ABOUT IT

Will the style of your invitation be formal or informal? Will it be in the form of a card, a letter, or another type of written communication? How will you decorate it? Will your decoration relate to the theme of the exhibit? Who was involved in preparing the exhibit? Where will it take place? When will it take place? Who should attend? Why should they attend? Who are a few of the featured characters? Who is in charge? Will refreshments be served? Is a response to the invitation required?

GET ORGANIZED

Plan your invitation. Explain the reason for the invitation in the form of a purpose statement. Fill in the who, what, where, when, why, and how information to help you develop your ideas. Use words, phrases, and/or short sentences. You can develop your writing into more complete, fluent sentences in the Compose section.

Purpose Statement: ____

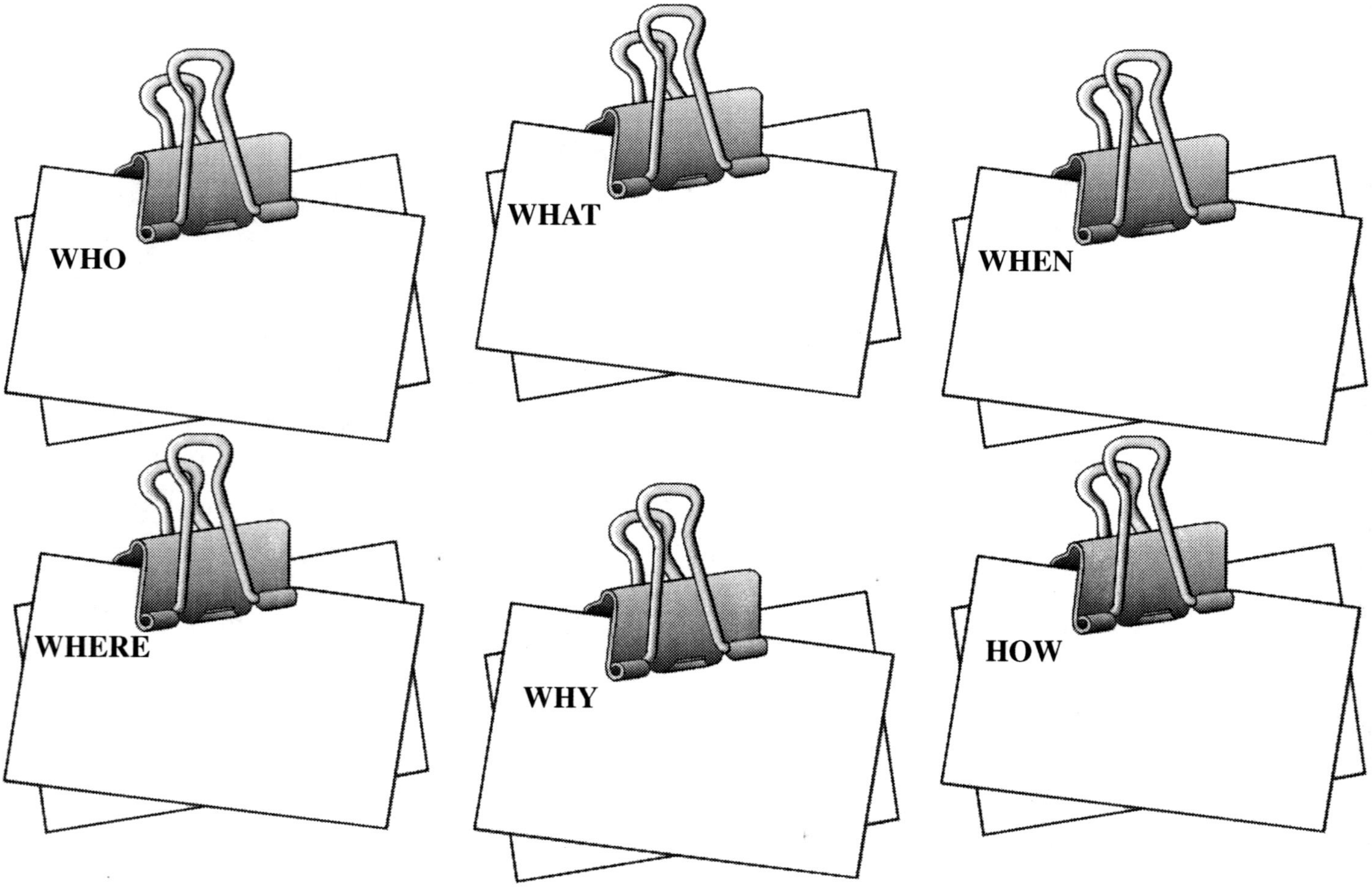

A Literary Wax Museum

COMPOSE

Clearly explain the reason for the invitation. Remember to include the necessary who, what, when, where, why, and how information in your expository writing. Refer to your writing ideas from the pre-writing section to get started.

REVISE

Edit your invitation by using the Writer's Checklist and the Editorial Symbols sheets. Then exchange papers with your pre-assigned writing partner. Each of you will use the same sheets to offer suggestions for improvement to the other. Now you are ready to rewrite your work in good form on another paper. Share the invitation with the whole class.

FOR MORE FUN

Pretend that your class is planning a similar exhibit. Gather in small groups to brainstorm a list of characters you might want to include from favorite books that you have read. Compare your list with those of other groups.

Trees Are Helpful

TOPIC

Your class has learned about different types of trees and their usefulness to humans. As a homework assignment, you have been asked to write a report on how trees are helpful.

THINK ABOUT IT

What foods are produced by trees? What non-food products do we get from trees? How do trees help your enjoyment of leisure time? In what other ways do trees help us? What resources might you use to help you in your research?

GET ORGANIZED

Plan your expository writing. Begin by writing an opening statement. It will act as a guide for you. Use words, phrases, and/or short sentences. You can develop your writing into more complete, fluent sentences in the Compose section.

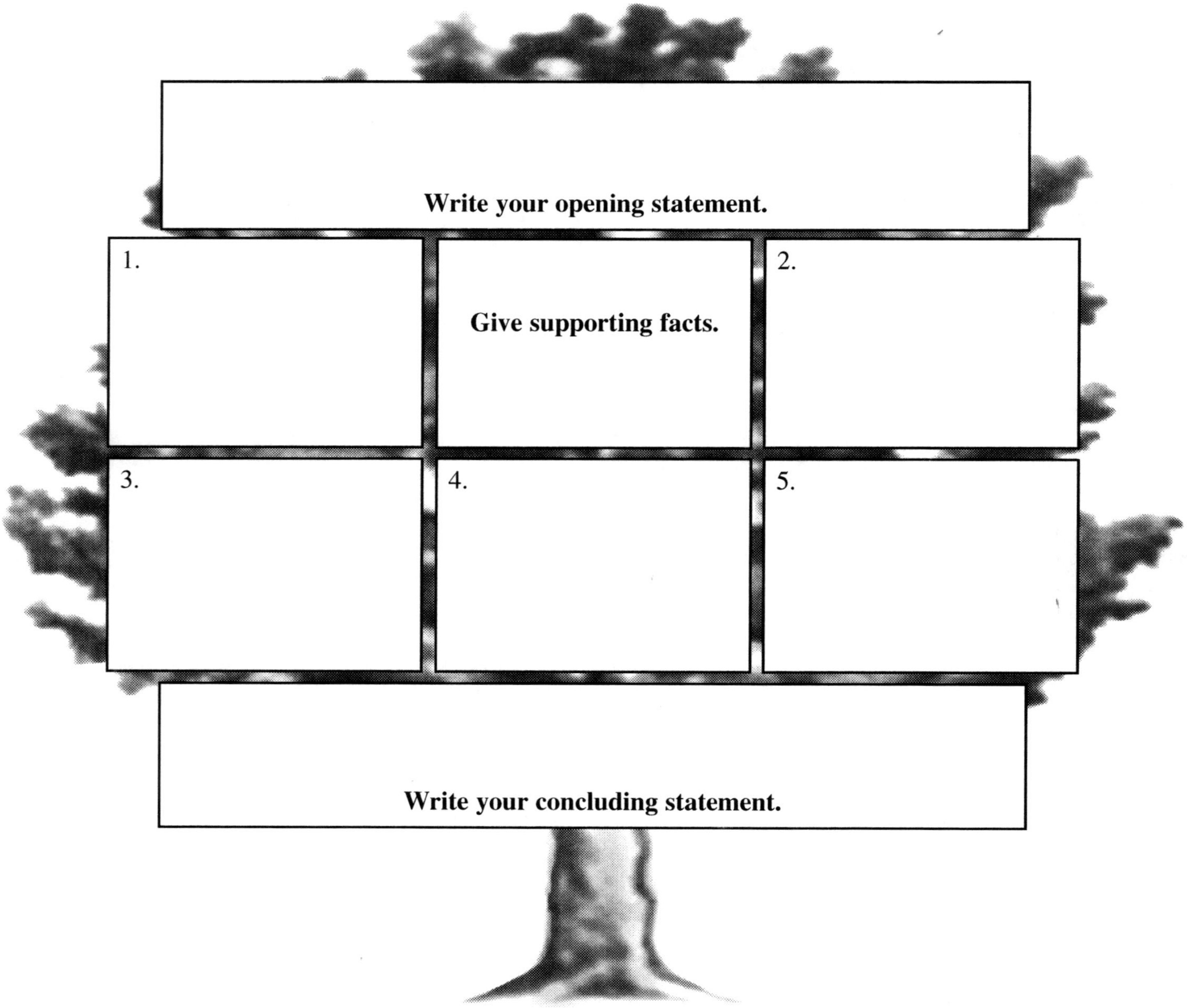

Trees Are Helpful

COMPOSE

Remember to write your expository writing about trees in sequence. For each paragraph use a topic sentence to state your main idea. Develop that idea by explaining different aspects of it and giving examples of each. Be sure to keep to the topic. Restate your main idea in your concluding sentence. Refer to your writing ideas from the pre-writing section to get started.

REVISE

Edit your report by using the Writer's Checklist and the Editorial Symbols sheets. Then exchange papers with your pre-assigned writing partner. Each of you will use the same sheets to offer suggestions for improvement to the other. Now you are ready to rewrite your work in good form on another paper. Share your report with the whole class.

FOR MORE FUN

Collect magazine photographs of the products derived from trees. Use them to create a poster-size montage. The posters may be displayed in the media center or on classroom bulletin boards.

Getting to the Reunion

TOPIC

Your parents are hosting a family reunion. Some of your relatives do not know how to get to your home. Your parents have asked you to prepare directions for those relatives.

THINK ABOUT IT

From where will your relatives be traveling? What means of transport will they be using? From what point will you begin your directions? Why? What landmarks can you use?

GET ORGANIZED

Plan your directions. Fill in the boxes with the streets, turns, and other directions you will give. Be sure to keep the steps in proper sequence. Include a landmark for each. Use words, phrases, and/or short sentences. You can develop your writing into more complete, fluent sentences in the Compose section.

Starting Point

Landmark:

1.

Landmark:

2.

Landmark:

3.

Landmark:

4.

Landmark:

5.

Landmark:

6.

Landmark:

Ending Point

Description of your home:

Getting to the Reunion

COMPOSE

When giving directions for going from one place to another, you must be very clear. Be sure to keep your directions in the proper sequence. Use sequence and distance words and phrases to clarify your directions. Remember to keep your sentences short. Do not include any unnecessary information. Check your directions by reading them from your readers' point of view. Refer to your writing ideas from the pre-writing section to get started.

REVISE

Edit your directions by using the Writer's Checklist and the Editorial Symbols sheets. Then exchange papers with your pre-assigned writing partner. Each of you will use the same sheets to offer suggestions for improvement to the other. Now you are ready to rewrite your work in good form on another paper. Share the directions with the whole class.

FOR MORE FUN

Create a map of your written directions. Include full-color illustrations of the landmarks to incorporate into the map or to accompany the map.

The Useful Atlas

TOPIC

Your class has just completed a month of map-study skills. As part of your final project you have decided to write a report on the usefulness of an atlas.

THINK ABOUT IT

What is an atlas? Are all atlases the same? If not, how do they differ? In what ways has an atlas helped you? Have you ever used an atlas to help you in a school assignment? In what other situations might an atlas be useful?

GET ORGANIZED

Plan your expository writing. Begin by writing an opening statement. It will act as a guide for you. Use words, phrases, and/or short sentences. You can develop your writing into more complete, fluent sentences in the Compose section.

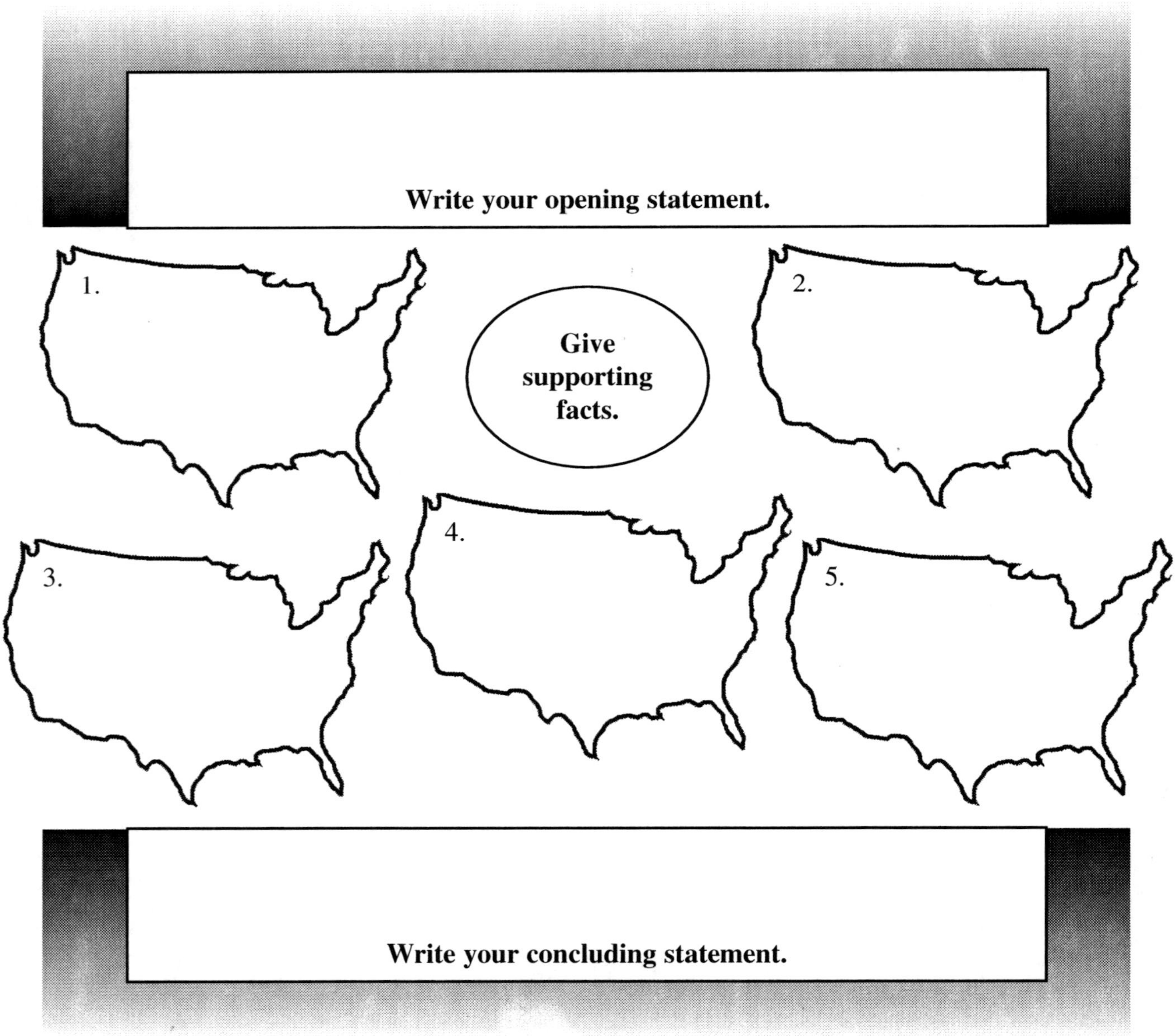

The Useful Atlas

COMPOSE

For this expository report you will write about the usefulness of an atlas. Use examples, comparison, definition and explanation, and/or cause and effect to develop your writing. Remember to begin each paragraph with a sentence that clearly states your main idea. Include at least three sentences that contain supporting details. Refer to your writing ideas from the pre-writing section to get started.

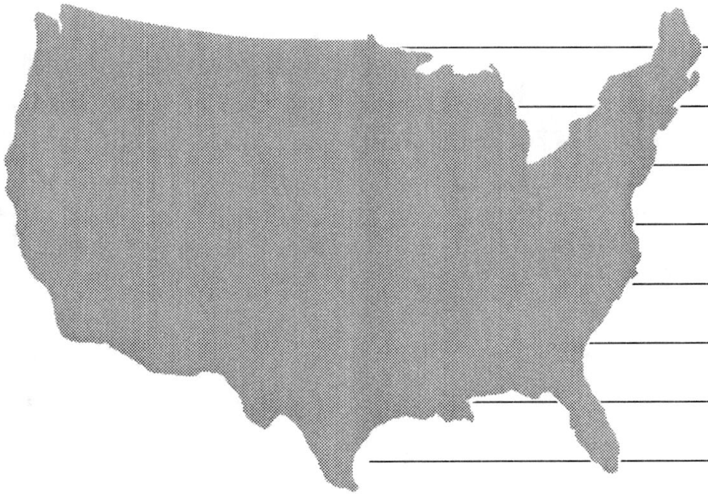

REVISE

Edit your report by using the Writer's Checklist and the Editorial Symbols sheets. Then exchange papers with your pre-assigned writing partner. Each of you will use the same sheets to offer suggestions for improvement to the other. Now you are ready to rewrite your work in good form on another paper. Share the report with the whole class.

FOR MORE FUN

Design a tabletop display of maps, globes, and atlases.

California Gray Whales

TOPIC

Gray whales were protected by law from 1946 to 1993 as an endangered species. They grow to about 47 feet and weigh up to about 70,000 pounds! Each year they migrate. Many people enjoy taking boat trips to see these migrating whales. Create a flyer for people about to take one of these trips. In it explain the migration of these fascinating animals.

THINK ABOUT IT

When do they migrate? Why do they migrate? Where do they migrate? How long does the migration take? Do they travel alone or in groups? Are they in danger as they migrate? Do they encounter any problems?

GET ORGANIZED

Plan your flyer. A clear opening sentence will help capture your readers' interest. Use words, phrases, and/or short sentences. You can develop your writing into more complete, fluent sentences in the Compose section.

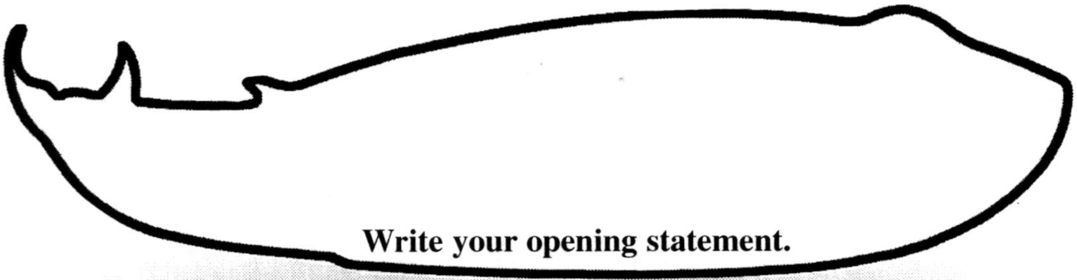

1.

Give supporting facts.

2.

3.

4.

5.

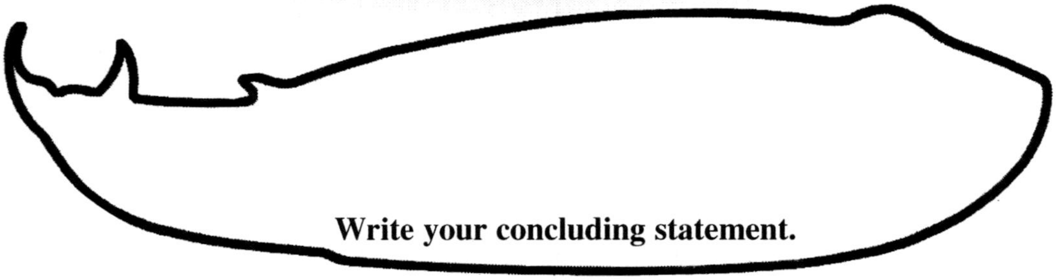

California Gray Whales

COMPOSE

Your expository writing will explain the migration of gray whales. Each paragraph in your report should have a clearly stated main idea and at least three sentences with facts to support it. Develop your writing by using examples, comparison, definition and explanation, and/or cause and effect. Be sure to keep your facts in the proper sequence and to stick to the topic. Refer to your writing ideas from the pre-writing section to get started.

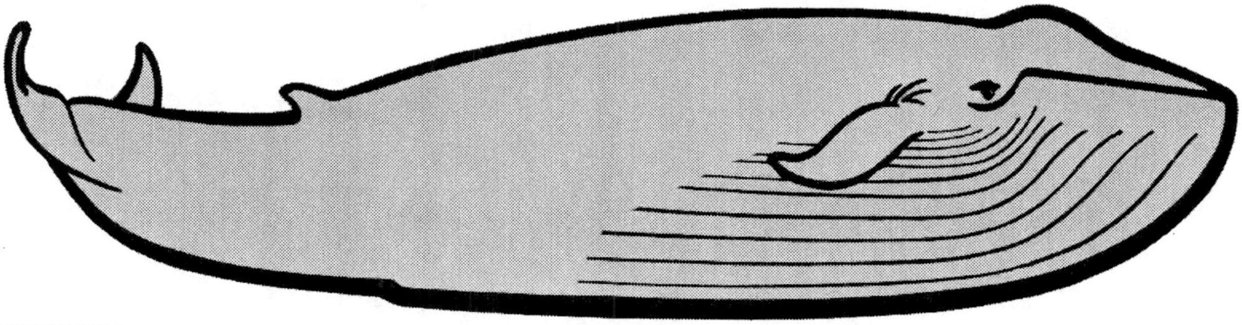

REVISE

Edit your flyer by using the Writer's Checklist and the Editorial Symbols sheets. Then exchange papers with your pre-assigned writing partner. Each of you will use the same sheets to offer suggestions for improvement to the other. Now you are ready to rewrite your work in good form on another paper. Share the flyer with the whole class.

FOR MORE FUN

Design the ticket one might buy for a whale-watching boat trip. Design a souvenir T-shirt for the passengers.

Cereal Boxes

TOPIC

Cereal boxes contain a lot of information: nutrition data, ingredients, calories, and more. Create an imaginary cereal. Write information to be included on the back of the box. Be sure to include a paragraph explaining why this cereal can be part of a healthy, balanced diet. Then add other useful information.

THINK ABOUT IT

Study some cereal boxes. What information is included? Is any information lacking that you wish were there? What are the ingredients in your cereal? Is it natural? Is it low in cholesterol? Is it sugar free or is it sweetened? Who is more likely to want your cereal, children or adults? Do you want to have a slogan for your cereal? Are you offering any special premiums or contests?

GET ORGANIZED

Plan your expository paragraph for your cereal box. A clearly stated opinion makes a good topic sentence. Use the five boxes on this page to record information and ideas in logical order. Check your facts and supporting details for accuracy. Restate your opinion in the concluding statement.

Name of Cereal: ______________________________

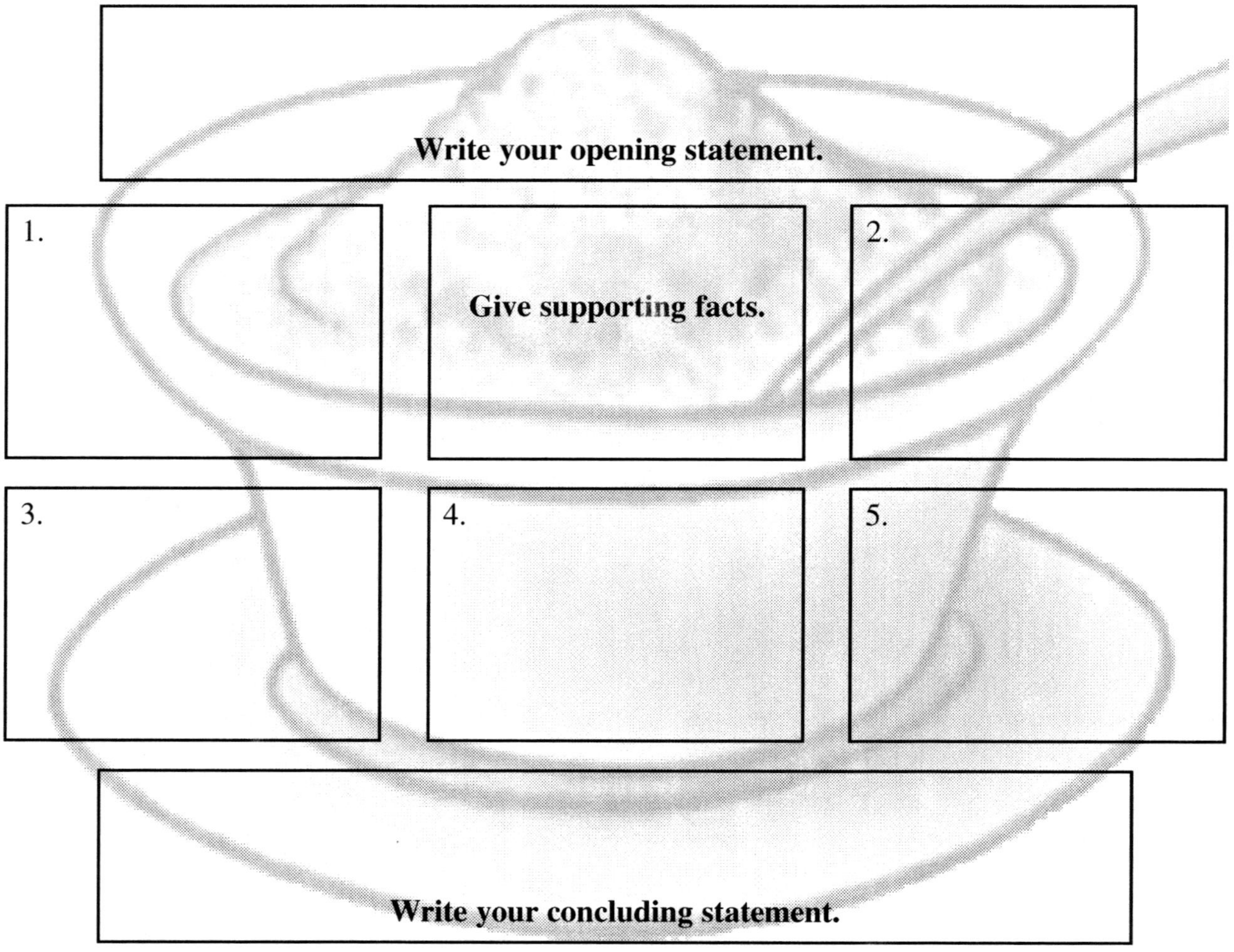

Cereal Boxes

COMPOSE

Begin your expository writing with a paragraph explaining why your cereal is an important part of a balanced diet. Your paragraph should have a clearly stated main idea and at least three sentences with facts to support it. Develop your paragraph by using examples, comparison, definition and explanation, and/or cause and effect. Then write the blurbs, slogans, and nutritional information you want to include on your box. Refer to your writing ideas from the pre-writing section to get started.

REVISE

Edit your writing by using the Writer's Checklist and the Editorial Symbols sheets. Then exchange papers with your pre-assigned writing partner. Each of you will use the same sheets to offer suggestions for improvement to the other. Cover an actual cereal box with construction paper. Rewrite your work in good form and paste it on your cereal box. Include the paragraph, nutrition facts, slogans, and other information you have written. Add illustrations. Share your writing with the whole class.

FOR MORE FUN

Create a jingle, or short poem, to advertise your new cereal. Make a tabletop display of the cereal boxes and jingles.

Mythical Explanations

TOPIC

The ancient Greeks had a myth to explain the growing seasons. It suggested that Demeter, the goddess of agriculture, was too upset to keep things growing during the months that her daughter Persephone had to spend in Hades. Write your own short myth to explain a natural occurrence.

THINK ABOUT IT

What natural occurrence will your myth explain? Consider rainbows, meteors, sunrise, sunset, earthquakes, snow, and so on. Who will be the main characters? How will you name them?

GET ORGANIZED

Plan your myth. Write a clear opening sentence to help capture your readers' interest. Fill in the who, what, where, when, why, and how information to help you develop your ideas. Use words, phrases, and/or short sentences. You can develop your writing into more complete, fluent sentences in the Compose section.

Natural Occurence Being Explained:______________________________

Opening Sentence: ____________________________________

____

Mythical Explanations

COMPOSE

Your expository writing will be in the form of a myth to explain a natural occurence in a non-scientific way. Write a topic sentence that clearly states your main idea. Remember, it is important to keep your facts in the proper order. Use time-order and space-order words to help make the sequence clear. Be sure to include all the information necessary to ensure that your readers understand the explanation. Create a title for your myth.

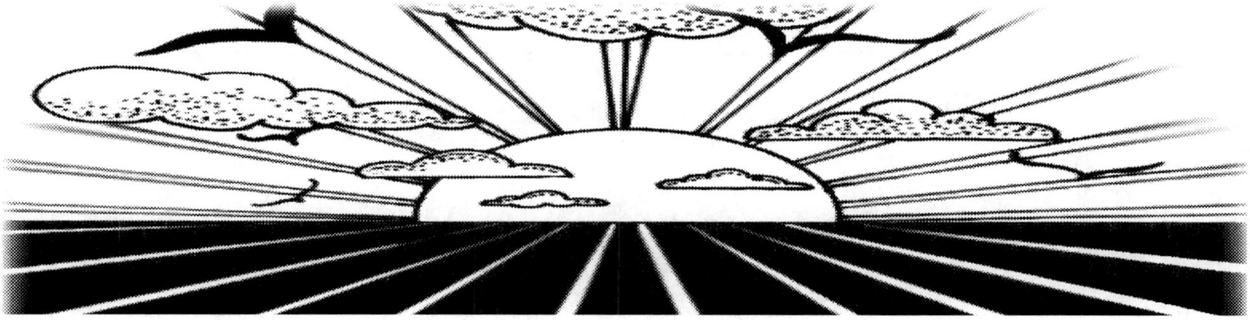

REVISE

Edit your myth by using the Writer's Checklist and the Editorial Symbols sheets. Then exchange papers with your pre-assigned writing partner. Each of you will use the same sheets to offer suggestions for improvement to the other. Now you are ready to rewrite your work in good form on another paper. Share your story with the whole class.

FOR MORE FUN

Create a full-color illustration for your myth.

Personal-Appearance Announcement

TOPIC

A hugely popular sports or television personality has agreed to visit your school. As a member of the committee to organize the event, your job is to prepare the flyer that will be posted around the school and in other public places.

THINK ABOUT IT

Who will be coming to your school? Why is he or she famous? Why is this celebrity coming? When is he or she coming? What will the celebrity do? Will the person be interviewed? Will he or she give a speech? Should the audience prepare in any special way? Will the audience be limited? What other information needs to be shared by way of this flyer?

GET ORGANIZED

Plan your flyer. Decide upon a good headline. Write a clear opening sentence to help capture your readers' interest. Fill in the who, what, where, when, why, and how information to help you develop your ideas. Use words, phrases, and/or short sentences. You can develop your writing into more complete, fluent sentences in the Compose section.

Heading: ______________________________

Opening Sentence: ______________________________

____

WHO

WHAT

WHERE

WHEN

WHY

HOW

Personal-Appearance Announcement

COMPOSE

Your expository flyer will be used to announce the appearance of the well-known personality. Include a headline and an interesting opening sentence to capture your readers' attention. Also include brief biographical information. Remember to include the necessary who, what, when, where, why, and how information about the event. Refer to your writing ideas from the pre-writing section to get started.

REVISE

Edit your writing by using the Writer's Checklist and the Editorial Symbols sheets. Then exchange papers with your pre-assigned writing partner. Each of you will use the same sheets to offer suggestions for improvement to the other. Now you are ready to rewrite your work in good form on another paper. Share the flyer with the whole class.

FOR MORE FUN

Create an acrostic poem about the personality you have chosen.

The Weather Report

TOPIC
You have been asked to write the weather report for your local radio or TV station. You may not realize it, but when you listen to a weather report, you are usually listening to the reading of a script. First the facts are gathered. Then the facts are used to write the script for the report.

THINK ABOUT IT
Before you begin, listen to a few actual weather reports. What weather information was included? Was the weather normal for the time of year? Was there a recent change in the weather? Was a drastic change expected? Were there any severe-weather warnings? What period of time was included? Did the report cover a small region or a large one? What else was included? For example, did the reporter introduce himself or herself?

GET ORGANIZED
Plan your weather report. Begin with a clear opening sentence to capture your listeners' interest. Fill in the boxes with types of weather data, facts about current weather conditions, and any changes which are expected. Use words, phrases, and/or short sentences. You can develop your writing into more complete, fluent sentences in the Compose section.

Write your opening statement.

1.

Give supporting facts.

2.

3.

4.

5.

Write your concluding statement.

The Weather Report

COMPOSE

In writing the monologue for your weather report, be sure to keep the facts in the proper sequence. Use time-order and space-order words and phrases which help clarify the sequence. Refer to your writing ideas from the pre-writing section to get started.

REVISE

Edit your weather report by using the Writer's Checklist and the Editorial Symbols sheets. Then exchange papers with your pre-assigned writing partner. Each of you will use the same sheets to offer suggestions for improvement to the other. Now you are ready to rewrite your work in good form on another paper. Share the report with the whole class.

FOR MORE FUN

Create a visual aid to help you present your weather report.

Earthquakes

TOPIC

Earthquakes are powerful forces of nature. They occur in various places around the world. Your current-events class has just finished reading about a severe earthquake in Turkey. You have been given the assignment to write a report about the causes and effects of earthquakes.

THINK ABOUT IT

Read about earthquakes to learn more about them. Take notes as you read. What is an earthquake? What causes earthquakes? Can they be predicted? Are there any interesting statistics regarding earthquakes? What is the relationship between tsunamis and earthquakes? What type of damage do earthquakes cause? How are they measured?

GET ORGANIZED

Plan your report. A clear opening sentence will help capture your readers' interest. Use words, phrases, and/or short sentences. You can develop your writing into more complete, fluent sentences in the Compose section.

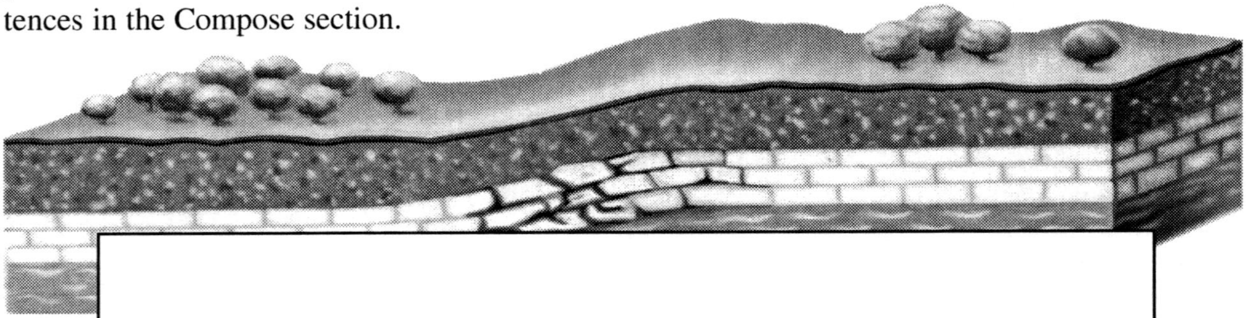

Write your opening statement.

1.

Give supporting facts.

2.

3.

4.

5.

Write your concluding statement.

Earthquakes

COMPOSE

Your expository writing will explain the causes and effects of earthquakes. Each paragraph should have a clearly stated main idea and at least three sentences with facts to support that main idea. Think about the various ways to develop your writing: examples, comparison, definition and explanation, and cause and effect. Refer to your writing ideas from the pre-writing section to get started.

REVISE

Edit your report by using the Writer's Checklist and the Editorial Symbols sheets. Then exchange papers with your pre-assigned writing partner. Each of you will use the same sheets to offer suggestions for improvement to the other. Now you are ready to rewrite your work in good form on another paper. Share your writing with the whole class.

FOR MORE FUN

Make a picture collage showing the effects of earthquakes.

How a Volcano Works

TOPIC

Your class has been studying the powers of nature. You have been assigned the task of writing an essay explaining the process of how a volcano forms and why it sometimes erupts.

THINK ABOUT IT

Think about the various cause-and-effect relationships involved in the formation and the eruption of a volcano. What resources will you consult for your research?

GET ORGANIZED

Plan your expository writing. A clearly stated opinion makes a good topic sentence. Use the thought webs on this page to record information and ideas in logical order. Check your facts and supporting details for accuracy. Restate your opinion in the concluding statement.

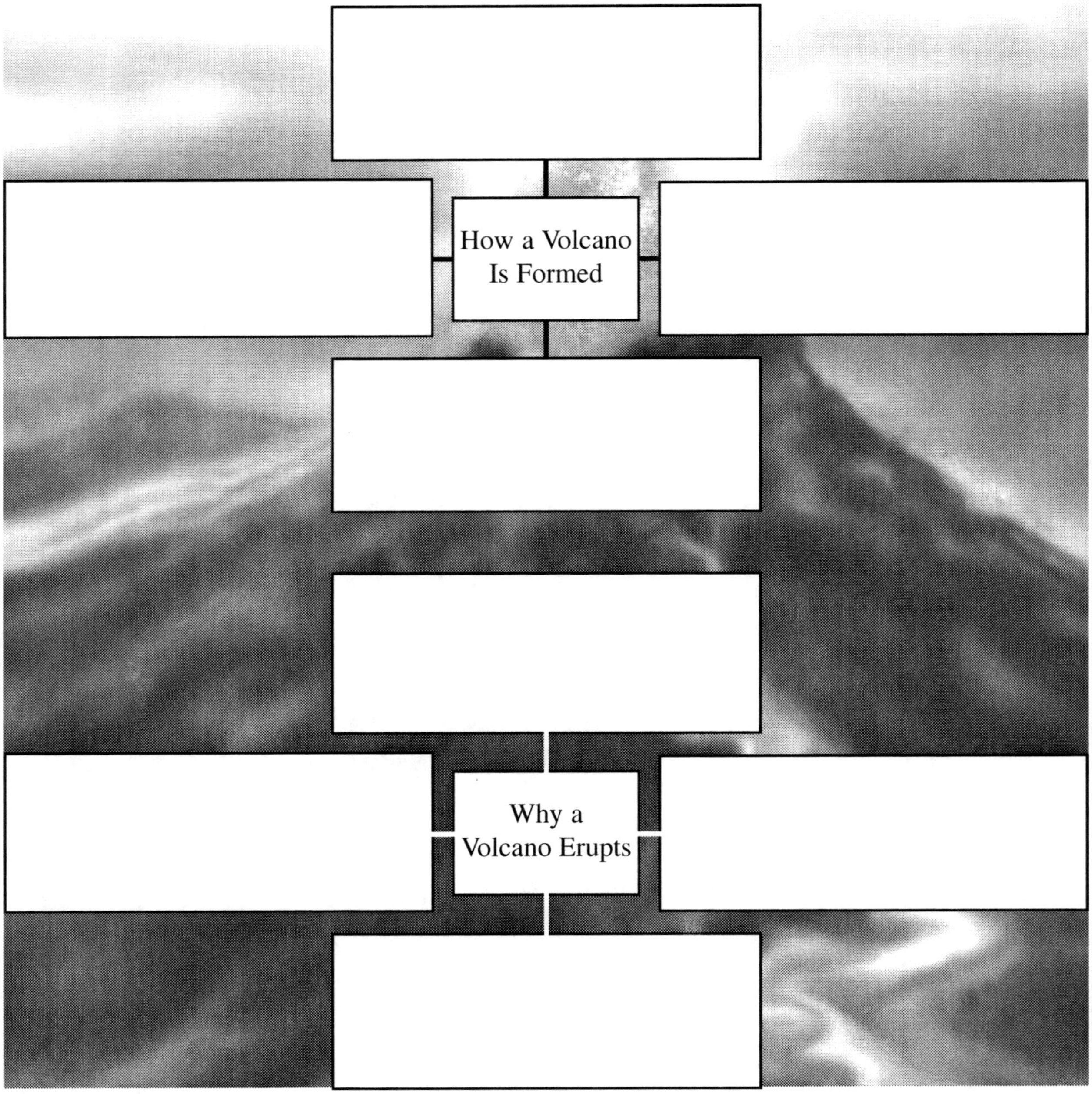

How a Volcano Works

COMPOSE

Your expository writing will be in the form of an explanation of the process of how volcanoes form and why they erupt. Each paragraph should have a clearly stated main idea and at least three sentences with facts to support your main idea. Think about the various ways to develop your writing: examples, comparison, definition and explanation, and cause and effect. Refer to your writing ideas from the pre-writing section to get started.

REVISE

Edit your report by using the Writer's Checklist and the Editorial Symbols sheets. Then exchange papers with your pre-assigned writing partner. Each of you will use the same sheets to offer suggestions for improvement to the other. Now you are ready to rewrite your work in good form on another paper. Share the report with the whole class.

FOR MORE FUN

Create a chart that enhances your explanation.

Comparing Baseball and Basketball

TOPIC

Your penpal from a foreign nation wants you to explain the differences between baseball and basketball. Write an explanation in your next letter. Compare and contrast the two sports in a way that is easy to understand.

THINK ABOUT IT

Even if you are familiar with the two sports, review the rules of each before beginning. What is the object of each game? In what type of facility is each game played? How many on a team? What special physical qualities or athletic abilities are helpful? How many on the field or court at the same time? In addition to the players, who is actively involved in the game? What equipment and uniforms are needed? In what season or seasons is each game played? How is the game scored? How many games in a season? Are there any special rules?

GET ORGANIZED

Plan your expository writing. Fill in the Venn diagram to help you. Place facts about baseball in the section on the left. Place facts about basketball in the section on the right. The middle section will include facts that pertain to both. Review the parts of a friendly letter. Use the facts to write your letter.

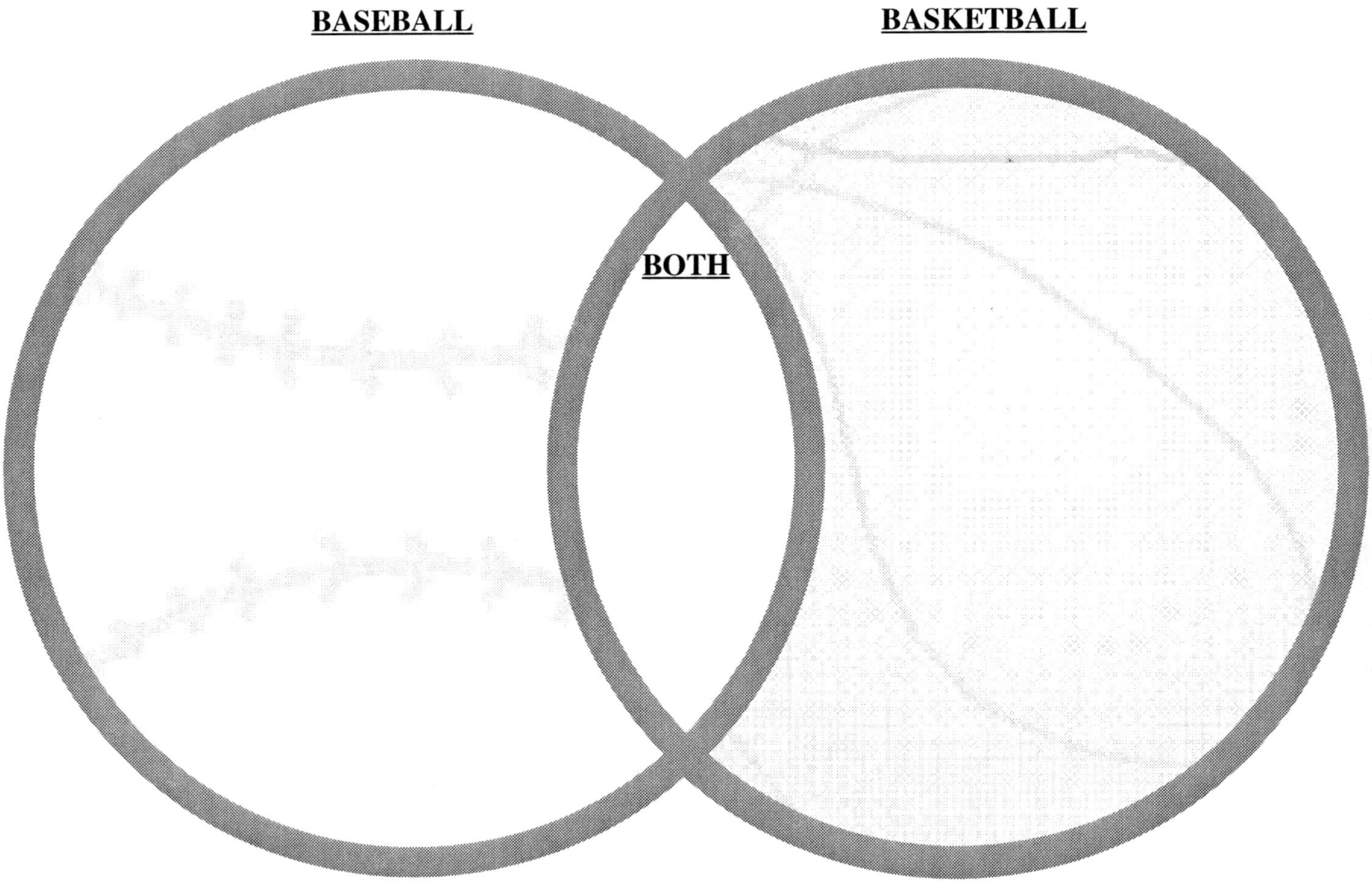

Comparing Baseball and Basketball

COMPOSE

Write a friendly letter to your penpal comparing and contrasting baseball and basketball. *Compare* by pointing out the likenesses between the two. *Contrast* by emphasizing differences. Each paragraph in your letter should have a clearly stated main idea and at least three sentences to support it. Refer to your writing ideas from the pre-writing section to get started.

HEADING: ______________________
____
____

______________________ **(GREETING)**

BODY: ______________________________________
____
____
____
____
____
____
____
____
____

CLOSING: ______________________

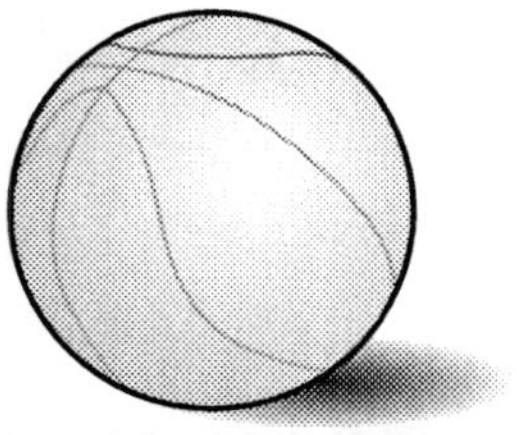

SIGNATURE: ______________________

REVISE

Edit your letter by using the Writer's Checklist and the Editorial Symbols sheets. Then exchange papers with your pre-assigned writing partner. Each of you will use the same sheets to offer suggestions for improvement to the other. Now you are ready to rewrite your work in good form on another paper. Share the letter with the whole class.

FOR MORE FUN

Create a Venn diagram comparing and contrasting two other activities.

An After-School Program

TOPIC

You are the student member of a committee to design a program to be held after school. You want your program to be the best possible. You must present your findings at the next meeting.

THINK ABOUT IT

Why are these programs important? What programs now exist in your school? What are some of your ideas for a new program? Which is your favorite idea? When should it be held? Where should it be held? Will it involve travel? What activities will members participate in? Who will supervise the program? Can anyone participate? If not, what qualifications are necessary? Why would this program be helpful?

GET ORGANIZED

Plan your expository writing. A clear opening sentence will help capture your readers' interest. Fill in the who, what, where, when, why, and how information to help you develop your ideas. Use words, phrases, and/or short sentences. You can develop your writing into more complete, fluent sentences in the Compose section.

Opening Sentence: ____

____

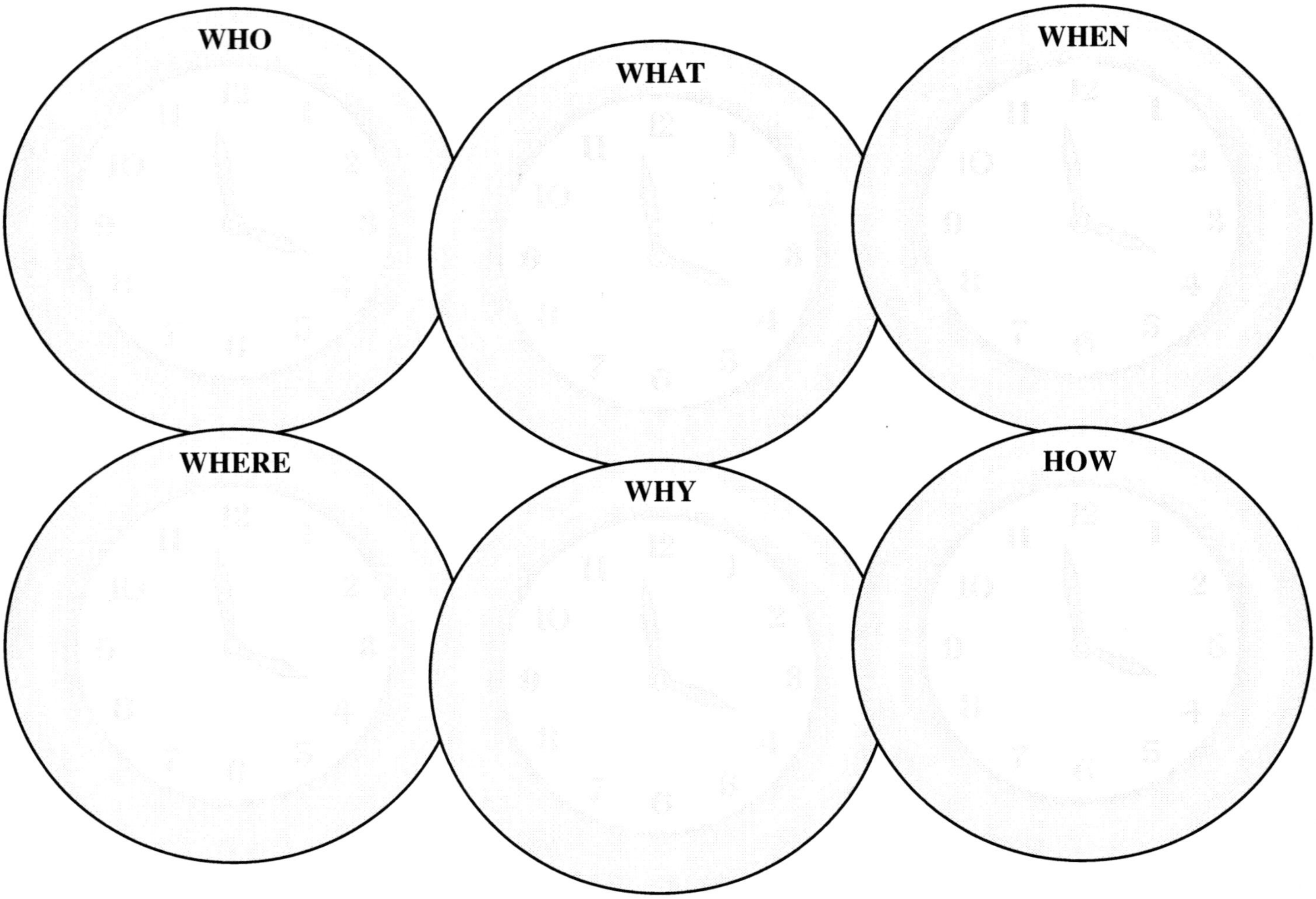

An After-School Program

COMPOSE

Plan your report to explain your idea for a before- or after-school program. Begin with an interesting opening sentence to capture your readers' attention and to tell your readers what kind of program you are suggesting. Remember to include the necessary who, what, when, where, why, and how information in your writing. Refer to your writing ideas from the pre-writing section to get started.

REVISE

Edit your writing by using the Writer's Checklist and the Editorial Symbols sheets. Then exchange papers with your pre-assigned writing partner. Each of you will use the same sheets to offer suggestions for improvement to the other. Now you are ready to rewrite your work in good form on another paper. Share your report with the whole class.

FOR MORE FUN

Collect pictures and drawings of activities that might be included in a before- or after-school program. Use the pictures to make a collage.

Additional Topic Ideas for Expository Writing

1. You have been assigned to watch a certain television program and to prepare a report about it.

2. There is a situation in your neighborhood that needs changing. Write an explanation of this in a letter to your local governing body.

3. Among your family and friends you are known as being very successful with horses. Write an explanation of how you handle certain behaviors of horses.

4. Write directions for programming the VCR to record one program while watching another.

5. Your class is preparing a time capsule for a new school. Items are being collected. Write an explanatory note that will be included in the time capsule.

6. Compare and contrast your current library-book selection with another book you recently read or compare two books by the same author.

7. Following a minor auto accident, your dog jumped out of the car. Write a notice about your lost dog. Include a drawing or photo with the other information.

8. There has been a drought in your region for some time. Explain the effects of the drought on your family, your community, wildlife, etc.

9. Your backyard attracts many types of birds. Use example to explain how to identify three different species.

10. Your class has planned a surprise going-away party for one of the students. Create an invitation for the party.